THE

STAR BOOK

FOR

MINISTERS.

BY

EDWARD T. HISCOX, D. D.,

AUTHOR OF " PASTOR'S MANUAL," " STAR BOOK SERIES,"
" HELPS TO PRAYER," ETC.

SIXTEENTH EDITION

REVISED AND ENLARGED.

PHILADELPHIA :

THE GRIFFITH AND ROWLAND PRESS.

1701 Chestnut Street

CONTENTS.

PREFACE.

THERE are various works now in use, intended especially to aid pastors in the incidental duties of their profession. These hand-books are convenient, and some of them valuable, as being well adapted to the purpose for which they were designed. But the conviction that one could be prepared which should be more largely serviceable for such purposes, than anything now accessible, has led to the preparation of the following pages. Whether this purpose has been realized, those who use it must decide for themselves.

The Scripture Selections for funeral and other occasions, constitute a leading feature in all such compilations. Clergymen who use an authorized liturgy will not need these; but for all others they will be found entirely sufficient, and it is hoped entirely satisfactory.

The compend of Parliamentary Rules, will be sufficiently full for all occasions in which clergymen are likely to take part. The rules given and statements of principles involved in the proceedings of deliberative bodies, are believed to be accurate and reliable, and in harmony with the best standards.

The forms of Marriage Service, including some long used by distinguished clergymen, have been given as at least suggestive to those who may still prefer to use their own—as very many ministers do. The forms of both marriage and burial service, of the Episcopal Church, have been introduced for the

benefit of those who, from personal preference or by special
request, may have occasion to use, in whole or in part, those
admirable forms.

The Scripture Proper Names, with their pronunciation and
signification, will be a special help to clergymen who may
at times have been subjected to peculiar perplexity for
want of the information conveniently at hand, which this
table furnishes.

The Forms and Blanks will be helpful to young ministers
particularly, in the correct arrangement of ecclesiastical matters, which they have frequent occasion to direct.

The tables of Facts and Figures constitute a new feature in
works of this kind. They have been compiled with considerable difficulty and with much care, and will be found as near
to positive accuracy as the subjects admit of attaining. Such
facts and figures, conveniently accessible, will be suggestive
of thought and remark, and furnish both argument and illus-
tration, especially welcome to clergymen on many occasions
besides those of their regular ministrations.

The work is commended to those for whom it has been prepared, in the hope that it may be a help to them, in the many
and varied, and often laborious duties of their sacred calling

                                                  E. T. H.

NEW YORK, Sept. 18, 1877.

SUGGESTIONS TO MINISTERS

IN RESPECT TO

WEDDINGS, FUNERALS, ORDINATIONS,

DEDICATIONS, RECOGNITIONS,

AND

OTHER SPECIAL SERVICES.

WEDDINGS.

MARRIAGE is both a civil and a religious institution. It has its legal relations, and is subject to and provided for by the enactments of civil law. But as divinely instituted, its moral and religious bearings are manifest. Its higher relations to the law of God are set forth in the Scriptures, and its nature, benefits and obligations are there explained and enforced.

1. Marriage as a civil contract consists in the parties making a declaration before competent witnesses that they take each other as husband and wife, pledging themselves to a faithful and life-long discharge of the duties reciprocally involved in that relation.

2. The persons designated by law to take the acknowledgment of the contract and make certificate of the same—to solemnize the bans—are regularly ordained and recognized clergymen of all denominations, justices of the peace, judges of courts, mayors of cities, and governors of states.

3. Marriage, solemnized by any person, if the parties properly make their declaration in the presence of competent witnesses, is valid in law; but the person who solemnizes the bans is subject to fine if he be not legally authorized to do it.

4. Divinity students, licentiates, and lay preachers

are not by law regarded as ordained clergymen, and cannot lawfully perform the marriage service.

5. As a social festival, the bearing and influence of the clergyman will go far towards giving it character. He is to remember that it should not be sad, solemn and oppressive, like a funeral, nor yet a scene of thoughtless and extravagant levity.

The one is as foreign to the true purposes of a wedding as the other. It should be cheerful, joyous, and inspiring, without losing the dignity and serenity of a social festivity sanctioned by religion. Its religious aspect is recognized in the fact that clergymen are usually sought for to solemnize the bans.

6. When the marriage takes place at the minister's own house, or in church, the occasion will be under his own control; when it is at the bride's home, he will not feel at liberty to interfere directly with the arrangements, and can only indirectly influence the occasion beyond his own official performance. His known wishes will, however, generally be respected.

7. The ceremony itself should not be so very brief as to seem trifling and unimpressive, nor yet so protracted as to be tedious and annoying. Extended counsel, however important, will be little considered during the excitement of such a service.

8. As to the form of the ceremony, the wishes of those to be united should be regarded, if they have any choice. If they have not, the clergyman will naturally proceed in his accustomed way.

9. One thing he should always do, strictly and conscientiously, viz., proceed without deviation *according to law*. No persuasion of friends, nor fear of losing a

fee, should induce him to violate legal enactments. Ministers of the gospel should be the last men to break the laws.

10. Nor, even where the law permits, should he unite in marriage persons whom he believes should not be so united. Run-away matches, and parties under suspicious circumstances, it is wiser to decline; prudence in this respect may save himself and others much trouble.

11. The minister should strictly question strangers, so as to satisfy himself that all is right. But those who would evade the law will be likely to evade the truth in such a case. In the state of New York the clergyman is now allowed to put the parties under oath, and to preserve their sworn and certified statement.

12. The law should be also strictly followed as to the registration of marriages, whether in city or country. Such laws are wise and salutary, and involve important interests.

13. Each clergyman will of course keep a private register of all marriages performed by him, with all essential particulars, for future reference and personal security, and at the same time give certificates of marriage to all parties desiring them.

14. As to the use of intoxicating drinks at weddings, those providing the refreshments will doubtless exercise their prerogatives in furnishing or omitting them. But the minister of Christ should never give any countenance or sanction whatever to their use at such a time. It would be worse than a blunder for him to allow himself to be per-

suaded to taste, or take, or in any way encourage so pernicious a practice.

15. It will be very proper for the clergyman to see the parties privately for a few minutes, previous to the ceremony, to obtain names, ages, &c., and to fill blanks, if the law requires such to be done. But especially that they may understand each other as to the ceremony, and thus avoid the likelihood of any blunder in its performance.

16. If through excitement, or inadvertence, any little mistake or blunder should occur, when the parties are on the floor, the clergyman should pass it off easily and pleasantly so as to relieve, as far as possible, the embarrassment that others might feel.

17. Especially should the minister himself avoid all mistakes, by being thoroughly self-possessed, and thoroughly familiar with the ceremony he uses, whether he reads it from a book or repeats it from memory.

18. When the marriage is in church, the ceremony may well be somewhat more formal and protracted than when in a private house, inasmuch as it takes on something more of the character of a public official, than of a private social service.

19. The minister should guard himself equally against unsocial reticence and flippant levity. The latter is the more to be shunned, since the tendencies are the stronger in that direction. And while he should be cheerful and easy, he should not sacrifice the dignity of his office to the festivity of the occasion.

20. Attendance at weddings often opens to the pas-

tor new opportunities of usefulness, which he should not fail to improve. By subsequently calling, not only on the newly married pair, but on their relatives, he may often spiritually benefit individuals, and perhaps win new families to his congregation.

21. The question has frequently been raised, whether ministers may properly unite in marriage persons who have been divorced for other causes than adultery. There are many and good men on both sides of this question; and whichever side one may take, he will find himself in good company. There can be no doubt that the rule given by our Saviour, in Matt. v., is the rule of Christian morality. But whatever views the minister may have as to extreme cases, he should always hold inviolate the sanctity of the marriage relation. He should never allow himself, by word or deed, to favor or further the loose notions respecting it which so frequently prevail, and according to which divorces are often procured by the most unworthy means, and under the most trivial pretenses. Marriage is too sacred an institution, and too vitally connected with the best interests of society, to be sacrificed at the demand of lust, caprice, or self interest.

FUNERALS.

THE visitation of the sick and attendance on funerals constitute a large item in the list of pastoral duties. And if faithfully attended to, they make a very serious demand upon both the time and energy of a Christian minister. Attended to faithfully, they certainly should be; because in this direction lies the path of duty, and because he never gains so ready access to the hearts of the people, whether for counsel or consolation, as in their times of trouble.

The minister is seldom consulted as to the time, place, or conditions of funerals. Usually, the arrangements are all made before he is notified and requested to attend. This is a mistake. He ought to be conferred with in respect to the matter, before the arrangements are fixed.

The following suggestions may be of use:

1. It is desirable that funeral services be held in the church, rather than in a private house, where the attendance is expected to be large, and more particularly if the private house be not commodious. At the church, all can be comfortably seated, and listen without inconvenience to whatever may be said. At a private house this is difficult, if not impossible, with any considerable number present.

2. At private houses, considering the inconven·
ience of the audience—sitting in uncomfortable posi·
tions, standing, some outside and some not hearing
the speaker—the service should be brief, seldom
exceeding thirty or thirty-five minutes.

3. Very unreasonable and sometimes very absurd
demands are made upon the officiating clergyman, as
to the position he shall occupy while performing the
service. The undertaker, or some friend of the family, informs him that he had better stand in the hall,
so as to be heard in all the rooms; though in the hall
he may be in a draft of air, liable to take cold, and
possibly himself to become the subject for a funeral,
besides the annoyance of being disturbed by persons
coming in and going out. Or he may be desired to
stand in a doorway between two rooms, so as to see
neither. Or, worse still, he may be placed half way
up the stairs, so as to be heard both above and below stairs, though he may have to talk to the wall,
the baluster, or to empty space and an imaginary
audience. Now, the minister should select the place
to stand which best suits himself, yielding only so
far as may be consistent to the wishes of friends.

4. Clergymen who use a prescribed liturgy have the
order and matter of service arranged, and will sel·
dom depart from them. Others will arrange the service according to their sense of propriety. It may be
supposed, however, that reading portions of Scripture, remarks, and prayer, will constitute the three
essential and unvarying elements of the service.

The most natural, and presumably the most com·
mon order, is this: Reading selected portions of

Scriptures; remarks on the occasion, and address to the mourners; prayer to close, with perhaps the benediction. Some may offer prayer to open and also to close the service. Singing may properly be introduced when convenient, particularly if the service be in church.

5. Preaching funeral sermons is not expected, except on rare occasions. When on account of the prominence of the deceased, or for other reasons, it may be desirable, the better way is, to have it take the place of a regular service on the Sabbath, and in the church; if that be not convenient at the time of burial, a brief service can be held at that time, and the sermon be preached at a subsequent time, notice to be given accordingly.

6. The custom, now much prevailing in cities and larger towns, of having the mourners sit up stairs, secluded, and entirely out of sight of the speaker, during a funeral service, is much to be condemned. Where such usage prevails, the speaker may talk about them, and pray for them, but cannot be expected to address those whom he cannot see, and who may not even hear what he does say.

7. It is bad taste and bad policy both, for a minister to harrow up the feelings of relatives by dwelling on the most sorrowful circumstances, in order to make the service affecting and impressive. But the most distressing features, if referred to, should be mentioned tenderly, and for the purpose of giving counsel or consolation.

8. Remarks at such a time are for the living, not for the dead. The virtues of the departed may appro-

priately be mentioned, especially if they have been conspicuous; but not in terms of extravagant laudation. Nor is it wise or prudent to specify and condemn, at such a time, the faults and sins of the dead. The great truths of Christian morality should no doubt be urged. But to offend and grieve afflicted friends, is no way to benefit them.

9. A clergyman will ascertain in some way, before he begins the service, the peculiar circumstances of the case, so as wisely to guide his remarks. Also concerning the near relatives of the deceased, whom he may be expected to remember in his prayer, if not in his remarks.

10. It will be proper, also, to speak personally to the principal mourners, both before and after the service—especially before, and particularly if they are strangers. A few kind words privately may give the minister more direct access to their confidence.

11. In cities and large towns it is not usually expected that the minister will go to the grave. It would be greatly inconvenient, and serve but little purpose. But where this service is usual, it is difficult for the minister to refuse, without offence, unless there be some excellent reason for so doing. If he does refuse, they will think him wanting in sympathy and consideration for the people in their trials.

12. When he does attend the burial it would appear proper for him to offer a very short prayer at the grave, or very brief remarks with the benediction. Thus his presence would mean more than a mere compliment to the occasion, or to the friends. But a service at the grave should be very short.

13. When the service is in church, it is usually expected—though not of course important—that the
minister shall walk up the aisle in front of the coffin.
Nor can there be any good reason why he should not,
at the same time, repeat appropriate scriptures,
after the manner of the Episcopal Service. When
the coffin is taken out, he would also walk in front of
it, to the hearse.

14. It seems quite unfortunate that funerals are so
generally arranged to take place on Sunday. They
impose a needless and severe tax on the time and
energies of the minister, on the day when he can
least afford it. They interrupt the ordinary services
of the day, and do not tend to the sacred observance
of the Sabbath. And yet special pains are taken to
fix them on that day, in order that they may be
largely attended, or that friends may save the time,
and not be interrupted in their secular pursuits.

15. The minister should take occasion to visit the
bereaved relatives in their homes, as soon after and
as often as convenient, in order that he may follow
up the lessons of Providence by his counsels, for
their spiritual profit. They are more likely to listen
to advice and receive spiritual comfort while under
the shadow of their afflictions.

VISITING THE SICK.

WHETHER a minister may or may not frequently call on his people at large, in pastoral visitation, no ordinary circumstances can excuse his
neglect of the sick. The sick room and the house in
sorrow constitute an imperious demand upon his
sympathies and his services. It is his duty, as the
shepherd of the flock. It is one of his broadest and
most inviting fields of usefulness.

It is undoubtedly true that not a few ministers dis-
like and shrink from this department of their work.
They claim that they are not adapted to it, and
cannot do it profitably. While it is true that visits
to the sick and dying may impose a painful obliga-
tion on some, especially young men, yet it can scarce-
ly be doubted that where such service seems repug-
nant, it is rather for want of a deeper and more fer-
vent piety, to bring the soul into a closer spiritual
sympathy with the suffering. The minister of Christ
who has the spirit of his Divine Master and of his
sacred calling, can carry the gospel as glad tidings
to the sick room, as well as proclaim it from the pulpit.
He will be a blessing, and will himself be blessed by
such a ministry. He can never be in full fellowship
with his calling until he can be the messenger of

consolation to the sick and dying. Such, let every
minister become.

1. Visits to the sick should be brief. How brief,
circumstances must determine, judged by the good
sense of the pastor. Protracted calls would consume
too much of his own time, and too much of the time
of the family, while they might harm rather than
benefit the patient.

2. As a general rule, it is better to visit the sick
during the forenoon, since they usually feel better,
and are stronger to bear any excitement in the early
part of the day. This is particularly true if they be
very feeble.

3. Much of the advantage of pastoral visits depends on the deportment and manner of the minister. He should approach the sick gently and quietly,
with a pleasant countenance, and with kind and gentle words. No true Christian gentleman will approach a sick-bed in a rough and boisterous manner,
and with a loud voice, as destitute of sympathy as it
is of courtesy. Nor should he come with a melan-
choly countenance, or with doleful and depressing
words.

4. The minister must remember that his visit is to
be a religious visit. It is for that purpose he is expected and desired to call. His conversation should
therefore be of a religious kind—hopeful, gentle, and
inspiring. No disinclination on the part of the sick
should prevent faithfulness in this respect, on his
part.

5. In many cases, especially of the unconverted, it
may be desirable for the minister to ask to see the

sick alone; since they may show their true religious state, and converse on religious subjects more freely alone than in the presence of others.

6. Persons very feeble should not be required to talk much. The effort, mental and physical, of conversing, and even of answering many questions, may be very exhausting. They can listen to conversation when they cannot converse. But if they desire to make statements, they should not be hindered, however feeble.

7. The minister should practice no deception on the sick, either as to their spiritual condition or in regard to the prospect of their recovery. It may not be best to express one's greatest fears as to recovery, but the sick should not be deluded with false hopes. The souls of backsliders and the unconverted should be dealt faithfully with—though always in kindness.

8. Prayer should almost always be offered; in which the condition of the sick can be mentioned, with even more plainness than in conversation. It should be brief, tender in spirit, and gentle in tone; and should embrace the members of the family, according to their condition, as well as the sick. Whether the whole family, with attendants, should be present at the time, must depend on circumstances. Sometimes this is impracticable. Sometimes it is better for the sick that but few should be present, to vitiate the air and confuse the sufferer.

9. A few brief and appropriate portions of Scriptures may well be read, preceding prayer; or what would prove quite as profitable, and perhaps less tiresome to the patient, let these appropriate portions be

repeated in the conversation; to which **brief com-**
ments may be added. Short, selected portions—single
verses, well chosen—will meet the condition of the
sick better, afford more instruction and comfort, and
be less tiresome, than entire chapters, or long con-
tinuous portions. The mental effort necessary to follow the reading of long passages is very considerable, especially if it be read rapidly, or indistinctly;
and is quite too much effort for a very sick person
to make.

10. It is fortunate if the minister can sing. If he
can sing well and wisely, his presence will be a special benediction in the sick-room. Song, soft and
sympathetic, inspires devotion, carries truth to the
heart as well as to the judgment, helps to lift the
soul into a spiritual atmosphere, and performs a ministry peculiarly adapted to such a service. But, better no singing than bad singing.

11. The whole manner, deportment and utterance
of one who visits the sick, should be calm, cheerful
and serene, assuring and not agitating the patient.
A noisy, harsh, and blustering deportment is as cruel
as it is discourteous, in the sick-room.

12. The minister should be very careful and not
intrude upon the province of the physician. Most
people have some favorite remedy of their own, for
almost every ill. From their great familiarity with
sickness, ministers necessarily obtain considerable
knowledge of diseases and remedies. But they
should carefully avoid playing the doctor. Their
sphere is chiefly spiritual. They may safely second
the physician's counsels as to careful nursing, pure

air, quiet surroundings, if there seems to be need of this. And if thoroughly satisfied that the sick are not receiving proper medical treatment, they may at times, no doubt, advise a change, and the procurement of a competent physician to attend them.

13. Clergymen in visiting the sick-room should avoid every possible condition of annoyance and discomfort to invalids. If their clothing be damp, the outside garment should be laid aside, or they should sit at a prudent distance from the bed. If the hands be very cold, avoid taking the hand of a very feeble patient. Some clergymen who use tobacco—what no clergyman ever should use—are so thoroughly saturated with its fumes, as to offend and almost nauseate even the well, much more the sick, whom they approach. Cases have been known where the sick and dying were obliged to exclude from their presence their own pastors, because the stench of tobacco upon their persons was unendurable, in their feeble condition.

14. The pastor will often—especially in cities and large towns—be called on to visit the sick in homes of poverty and want; perhaps in habitations of squalor and degradation. He must, so far as is in his power, preach to such a gospel of food and raiment, as well as a gospel of repentance and faith. Let him, as he is able, of his own personal means, relieve the wants of the sufferers. But he should enlist the kind services of the generous, to minister to such sufferers. Such charities will be doubly blessed: to those who give, as well as to those who receive. It will give the minister greater influence in spiritual work, among such families.

COUNCILS.

IT is usual on various occasions of ecclesiastical ac
tion, to convene councils for advice and co-oper.
ation. Ministers, as the chief actors in such bodies,
should understand the proper sphere of council action, and the true limits of council authority. Especially important is it for ministers to understand this,
since, though they are usually composed in part of
laymen, the clerical members are commonly in the
majority, and are supposed to take the lead of affairs
and give direction to the action taken. A few of the
leading features and principles are the following:

1. Councils have no antecedent right of existence,
and no original authority for action. Their existence
depends on those who convene them, and their authority to act is derived from the same source. No
company of persons, not a church, has the right to
convene themselves, organize and take action on ecclesiastical matters which have not been committed
to them.

2. Councils may be convened by churches or individuals—more commonly by churches—to give advice and aid in matters to be submitted to them
when convened.

3. Councils are usually convened by sending letters
to such churches as they may choose—a majority of
which should be those in the immediate neighbor-

hood—asking them to send their pastor, and one or two—usually two—messengers to sit in council with them. These letters are called *letters missive*, and constitute the only authority for the assembling of the body, and the charter under which it is to act, when assembled.

4. The *letters missive* should distinctly state when and where the council is to meet, and what churches and individuals are invited to attend.

5. The *letters missive* should also distinctly state what are the matters on which they are expected to act. It is an admitted principle, sanctioned by general usage, that an ecclesiastical council cannot be convened under a roving commission, to act on any subject that may chance to come up; but must confine its action strictly to the matters specified in the letters by which it was convened. Of course all those letters should be uniform. -

6. Parties cannot properly convoke a council to investigate or pass judgment on the case of persons with whom they hold no ecclesiastical connection; such as a member or pastor of another church than that with which those convoking the council are connected. But one church may call, and ask a council to advise them as to their duty in respect to some other church with which they are in fellowship.

7. It is not an uncommon practice for those calling a council, to invite, in addition to churches, certain ndividuals, whose presence may, for reasons, be desirable. To this custom, although it constitutes a somewhat mixed commission, there seems to be no reasonable objection.

3

8. Councils differ from Committees of Conference, in the fact that the former are composed wholly or chiefly of messengers appointed by churches, and the latter, of individuals personally invited, and acting without any church appointment.

9. The Council, when convened at the hour designated, organize by the election of some member as chairman, and some other one as clerk. These elections are usually on nomination. Prayer is then offered for divine guidance. After this the credentials of messengers are called for, and the clerk makes a list of members. Then the object for which the body is convened is stated—usually by reading a copy of the *letter missive*. By this the Council knows what it is desired to do. Further explanations, and a discussion of the subject then follow, concluding with such action as the body may decide on.

.10. A Council when organized can neither increase nor diminish the number of its members. Its composition is formed by those who called it, and cannot be changed by any other authority. For that reason it cannot admit other persons to membership, nor can it exclude any of those who have been called and appointed to constitute it.

11. But, as an exception to this rule, all deliberative bodies have the primal and inherent right to protect themselves against insult, disgrace, and such interruption as would prevent the object of their meeting. Such conduct on the part of any member, therefore, during the proceedings, would make his expulsion justifiable.

12. But if any member of a Council be dissatisfied

with the presence of any other member, he can himself withdraw, and refuse to act. He has no other
remedy.

13. Usage has not decided that any specified number of messengers appointed, shall constitute a *quorum*
essential for action. Any considerable number, or
even a very small number present, usually proceed to
action, especially if the case be one involving no
special difficulty. If the case be important and difficult, action should not be taken without a full rep-
resentation. In all important cases certainly, it would
be a salutary rule if adopted, that no action should be
taken, unless a majority of those actually called to
constitute the council were present. But so diverse
are the opinions of those who act on councils, as well
as those who have convened and desire them to act,
that no rule fitted to all occasions, can probably be
adopted.

14. It must be accepted as a fundamental and
universal rule, that within the area of Congregation-
alism and Church Independency at least, all councils
are *advisory* only; they never have, and cannot have
any ecclesiastical *authority*. They can only consider
such subjects as are submitted to them; and they
bind individuals and churches only so far, as they
choose to submit themselves to their judgment and
advice. Their province is simply *counsel*—what their
name implies; never and in no sense, are they
church courts for adjudication, much less legislative
bodies for the enactment of laws.

15. A council may adjourn from time to time, if
necessary to complete the purpose for which it was

convened.   But it cannot perpetuate a continued
existence, as a standing court of appeal.   When its
object is accomplished, it expires by limitation ; but
a formal vote to *dissolve*, or to adjourn *sine die,* is
usually passed.

16. Before adjournment, the minutes of the proceedings are read, corrected and approved, and a
certified copy is ordered to be given to the parties by
whom it was called.

17. When once dissolved or adjourned, the body is
extinct, and cannot convene again at its own option
or by its own authority.   If convened again, it must
be by the same authority, and by a process similar
to that which first brought it into existence.

18. It is not proper for one Council to sit in judgment on, or review the action of another Council.
But a matter, not satisfactorily adjusted by one, may
be referred to a second.

19. When a second is called to consider some matter already submitted to a previous Council, the second should, so far as possible, embrace all the members of the previous one, with such additional members as will be likely to counterbalance any local or
personal prejudices or any want of information or experience, which may possibly have influenced the
former meeting.

20. A Council may be called by a single church,
or by several churches acting in concert ; or by a
single individual, or by several individuals acting in
concert.   The *letters missive* should of course distinctly state by whom the call is issued, as well as the object for which it issued.

21. Councils called to adjust and settle difficulties, are usually designated as either *mutual* or *ex parte.* A *mutual* Council is one as to which the different parties to the difficulty, unite in the call and reference. An *ex parte* Council is one called by one party to the difficulty.

22. An *ex parte* Council should not be called until all proper efforts have been made for, and failed, to secure a *mutual* Council.

23. Parties not uniting in calling a council, can have no rights or standing in the body when convened; but as a matter of courtesy, and for the sake of obtaining all possible information, they may be heard by consent of the body and those who called it.

24. Parties calling a Council cannot be members of it, and have no rights of action with it, except to place before the body all the information in their possession.

25. An *ex parte* Council, when convened, cannot by its own action transform itself into a *mutual* Council. This change can be effected only by the consent and agreement of the different parties involved in the difficulty.

26. When a *mutual* Council is to be called to adjust difficulties between a church and some of its members, the letters convening it should be sent out, by and in the name of the church, and not of the individuals. But the fact of its being by mutual agreement of the parties, should be stated in the letters.

27. A Council cannot sit to review and pass judgment on the action of any other church than that which has called, and submitted its case to it; nor

3*

can a Council properly be called for such a purpose. No body of men has the right to try, and pass judgment on an independent church. Such a body would thereby become judicial—a church court.

28. But either churches or individuals may call a Council to advise them what is their duty in relation to a church deemed heretical in doctrine, or irregular in practice; or for other reasons thought important.

29. Members when aggrieved by the action or attitude of their church, and failing to secure a mutual Council, before proceeding to call one *ex parte*, should lay the matter before some neighboring church or churches, and request them to call one, for advice, either to the aggrieved members, or to the churches calling it; or to both. This effort failing, the members can themselves proceed to issue a call.

30. If when invitations are received to unite in a Council, those receiving them do not approve the object of the call, and decline to act, they should at once notify the party calling it, to that effect, giving their reasons for non-concurrence. These facts should be laid before the body when convened. But it is better to respond, if the call be issued from any respectable source, and by one's presence prevent any unfortunate action, rather than permit it by absence.

31. It is a course of very questionable propriety, for a Council to require the parties to a difficulty to bind themselves at the beginning, to abide by whatever decisions the body may reach. For, it is hardly consistent with the rights of conscience to pledge one's self beforehand to a course of action contingent

on future and unforeseen events. And as a matter of fact, such pledges, when made, are seldom kept.

32. Councils for the adjustment of questions involving church action should not be called unless the need seems imperative. And against all tendency to relieve churches from their appropriate responsibility, to intrude upon the sphere of their just authority, or to undermine their absolute independence—against all this, Councils should constantly and sacredly guard.

ORDINATIONS.

ON occasions of the induction of candidates into the public and official work of the ministry, the counsel and co-operation of others is usually sought by the church whose minister is to be ordained. This is done not for the sake of authority, but for the sake of order; not because it is essential, but because it is customary, and moreover because it is expedient and wise to pursue such a course.

Any church has the undoubted right to have any man whom they may elect, serve them as pastor, without interference by any other man, or body of men whatever; and to ordain, or set him apart, by such formal services as they may choose, either with or without the assistance of any other persons than themselves. The presence of ordained ministers, though desirable, is not essential.

But as every church desires to stand in cordial relations of fraternity and fellowship with all the other churches of its denomination; and as the man to be ordained is about to take his place in the brotherhood of ministers, and desires to sustain relations of sympathy, fraternity and fellowship with them all, it is a wise and prudent course to call together messengers from the various churches to examine the matter, and advise as to the propriety of inducting the candidate into the ministry ; giving him their approval and commendation—if they do approve—as he enters the sacred office.

This is accomplished in one of two ways. Either by requesting a given number of churches to send messengers to constitute a *Council* for action in the case; or, by inviting certain ministers to come together as a *Presbytery*, and perform the service desired. As to which shall be done, is a matter of opinion and choice with the church and the candidate, and wholly a matter of indifference so far as the results are concerned. At the North, the Council is commonly chosen ; in the South, the Presbytery is usually preferred. As a matter of fact, ministers perform almost the entire service, though the Council may be composed in part of laymen.

1. The Council, or Presbytery, is to be called together by the church over which the candidate is to be ordained, and not by the candidate.

2. The candidate should be a member of the church calling the Council, and over which he is to be ordained.

3. The church, before calling the Council, should take all proper care and pains to be satisfied as to the fitness of the candidate for the important position he is about to assume, as their pastor. It is not simply the question as to whether he can interest an audience by a public discourse, but whether he gives evidence of having been called of God to the work ; whether he is fitted to instruct and build up the church ; his ability to conduct the social services ; his adaptation to pastoral work, and his prudence and

ability to be a wise and safe guide and leader of the people.

4. The church should also inform itself as to his general character, and reputation, and what has been his walk and deportment hitherto. For all this the church is responsible, and this duty should not be thrown upon the Council.

5. When the Council is convened, and organized, the church—which does not compose a part of the Council, but reports to it—through some one appointed to represent it, reports what action they have taken in the case, the information they possess, and ask the advice and co-operation of the Council, as to whether their action has been wise, and is to be approved.

6. The Council then proceeds to examine the candidate. This examination is usually in three specific directions.

a. As to his Christian experience.

b. As to his call to the ministry.

c. As to his view of Christian doctrine.

On each of these he makes his statement, and at the conclusion of each, is asked any questions, which any member of the body may see fit to propound.

It would not only be proper, but desirable, for the candidate to be examined on matters not specifically included in the above list. As for instance, what would be his treatment of certain matters of church difficulty, or perplexing questions of discipline, or any of the many practical matters with which a pastor has to deal.

7. A Council having accepted the position of advis

ers to the church, should be faithful to their convictions, and not allow themselves to act contrary to their best judgment, merely to please either the church or the candidate.

8. A young man may not have had opportunity to make himself familiar with the details of scholastic theology, but no man should assume to enter upon the important work of the Christian ministry, or be encouraged to do so, until he be grounded and settled in the fundamental truths of the Christian system. The work is too important and responsible. To say, " He will learn as he goes on," and that " He will come out all right," is to trifle with sacred things.

9. On some minor points a candidate may not be thoroughly settled, but if he have fixed opinions contrary to the standards of his denomination, either as to doctrine or practice, on matters deemed by the Council important, they should not approve his ordination, nor assist in it. For even on the assumption that he be right and they wrong, his induction into the ministry would introduce an inharmonious element into the denomination, and almost certainly lead to dissension and discord.

10. When the examination of the candidate is completed, he retires, and the Council deliberates by itself, and decides whether it approves of proceeding to ordination. If they do, they so determine, and notify the church, or its committee, to that effect. And as the church has referred the matter of public services to the Council, they proceed to make arrangements for the same.

11. Usual ordination services are in the following order :

a. Introductory services, consisting of **singing**, reading the Scriptures, and prayer.

b. The sermon; by some one usually previously selected for the purpose.

c. The ordaining prayer; during which the candidate kneels, and near the close of which the one who prays, with one or two others, lay their hands on his head.

d. The hand of fellowship; by which he is welcomed to the fellowship of the ministry.

e. The charge to the candidate; in which certain matters of duty and deportment are urged upon him.

f. The charge to the church. This is designed to impress upon the church their duties and responsibilities towards their pastor.

Singing may follow, and the benediction is pronounced, usually by the candidate.

12. It is proper for a certified copy of the minutes of the Council, embracing the order of exercise, to be given the candidate, as the certificate of his ordination.

13. It must be kept in mind that ordination does not make a minister of Christ. It endows him with no gifts, graces, or capabilities which he did not before possess. Nor does it impart any ecclesiastical authority; for those who ordain, have none to give. His call to the ministry must be from God; his call to the pastorate must be from the church. The ceremony of ordination is no more than a recognition of his divine calling to the work, an approval of the church's action and of his entrance upon the duties of the office; while the public ceremonies are **but**

an appropriate and an impressive public commendation of the candidate, sending him forth to his work with a fraternal benediction.

14. Nor is the form of public service by which a candidate is inducted into the office to which he had previously been chosen, important. The "laying on of hands" has usually been deemed essential to ordination. It has the force of long prevailing and widely extended usage. Moreover, it is, if rightly understood, an appropriate form of fraternal benediction. But there is no instance found in the New Testament in which a man was inducted into the gospel ministry by the imposition of hands; nor any precept enjoining it. It is not, therefore, of divine authority, and cannot be made essential to ministerial character or standing. But, since it is customary, and since uniformity of usage is desirable, the usual forms should be followed, unless they be regarded as a violation of conscience or of principle.

15. It may not unfrequently happen that a council, while recognizing the divine call of the candidate to the ministerial office, may yet be convinced that he is not fully prepared to assume the sacred functions, and enter at once upon the responsible duties of the position. He may need clearer views of divine truth, in order to be a safe teacher, and more maturity and experience in order to be a competent leader. The prudent and kindly course in such a case, would be for the council to adjourn, for so long a time as they might deem necessary, in order that he might at a later day give them entire satisfaction as to his preparation for the sacred office.

4

INSTALLATION.

INSTALLATION, though with some denominations it means a more formal and official act,
yet with independent churches, it implies an unof-
ficial service, by which a pastor is introduced to a
new field of labor. Installation services are not held
with any uniformity; indeed but few of the many
pastoral changes are attended by them.

They constitute a fraternal greeting to a pastor,
at his entrance upon a new field of labor, and bring
the new era of the church's history prominently before the community, by a public service. Beyond
this, they have no ecclesiastical significance.

No Council is called, and no examination is had;
but several ministers are invited in, to take part in
the services. Some one is selected to preach a sermon on the occasion; some one to give an address
of welcome to the newly elected pastor; and some
one to address the church, by way of congratulation
and counsel. This is substantially the form and
meaning of an installation service.

RECOGNITION, OR RE-ORDINA-TION.

WHEN a minister, having changed his ecclesi-astical views, enters the denomination, from some other communion, he is admitted to the ministry in his new religious connection, either by a *re-ordination* or a *recognition* service. Usage is not uniform, and so far as his ministerial character and standing are concerned, there is no difference which is chosen. Whichever the minister and the church should prefer, may well be adopted, without prejudice to either.

In either case a Council, or Presbytery, should be assembled, and the candidate pass a sufficiently careful examination to give assurance that in matters of faith and practice, he is in harmony with the denomination into which he is admitted. Otherwise, he cannot expect a cordial recognition by them.

The services in *re-ordination* are usually the same as those of ordination; while those of *recognition* differ only in omitting the laying-on of hands. The imposition of hands may safely be left to the candidate, the church, and the Council. The man will be a minister none the more by the use of this ceremony, and none the less by the omission of it.

Sometimes a church will admit to membership, and put into the ministry as its pastor, one received from another denomination, without Council for advice, or public ceremony. This, they have an undoubted right to do, but it is neither wise nor expedient; neither for the church nor for the pastor.

Whether ordination confers an indelible character, and he who is once a minister, is always a minister, or, whether the ecclesiastical acts of one denomination are to be recognized as valid by another, are questions of no great practical moment, and in respect to which opinions widely differ. They can be settled by no authoritative decision, and may safely be left to the disposition of those with whom they may chance to arise. It is, however, better for each denomination to conform to its own polity, and follow its own order. It implies no want of Christian courtesy and suggests no disrespect, that the acts of one are not accepted as valid by another.

RECOGNITION OF CHURCHES.

WHEREVER there may be living near each other a number of Christian disciples, who entertain like views of Scripture doctrine and church order, it is their privilege to organize themselves into a church, by entering into covenant to be a church for the purpose of observing the ordinances of religion, and maintaining public worship. Such a company of believers, if they are members of churches already, would obtain letters from their churches, for this purpose. If not members, they would seek baptism, and make a public profession of their faith, preparatory to entering into the constitution of a church.

And such a company of believers, so becoming a church by uniting in covenant together, are in fact a church, possessing all the rights, privileges and authority of a church of Christ, without the sanction, permission or authority of any man, or body of men whatever, aside from their own number. No person or persons have a right to hinder, or interfere with them in the exercise of these rights.

But since churches of like faith and order, wish to be in fellowship with other churches of similar faith and order, and to exercise the courtesies of Christian fraternity towards each other, it is customary for

4*

one, when it is constituted, as above, to invite a Council, to look into the circumstances, and give their approval—if they do approve—of the step they have taken in their organization. And thus also, to express fellowship for them, as a regular and properly constituted church of Christ.

The Council usually examines their articles of faith, to see if they are in harmony with the denomination, as to doctrine and church order. They also consider whether a church be needed in that locality : whether the members could not be accommodated with religious privileges without the constitution of a new church ; and whether they have promise of being able to sustain worship, and meet the expenses to be incurred.

The approval of a Council secures for the new body the confidence and sympathy of other churches, and gives them credit in the denomination. But should the Council refuse their commendation and disapprove the organization, still they would be a church, and possess all the rights of one, did they choose to maintain their position. But in such a case they would not be likely to command the public confidence.

Some public *recognition* services are usually held, to give expression to the approving action of the Council. These generally consist of a sermon and addresses of welcome, encouragement, and counsel to the church, the people, and the pastor—if there be a pastor.

In the opinion of some, the proper time for calling a Council is before the organization of the church takes place, and not afterwards. The Council can then advise whether it is best that a church should be formed, rather than to express approval or disapproval of the act after it is accomplished.

The action in such cases, as in others, is **advisory, and not authoritative.**

LAYING A CORNER-STONE.

THE construction of church edifices—and often, of other buildings designed for religious or benevolent purposes, or even for special public use—is signalized by the ceremony of *laying the corner-stone*. The significance of the service is supposed to be, a declaration of trust in God for the success of the work, which is professedly for His praise; and on the enterprise His blessing is invoked.

The corner-stone itself, is a block usually different from the material of the foundation in which it is placed. On the front of it the year in which it is laid is engraved in figures.

A vertical cavity is made in the stone sufficiently large to hold a metallic box, in which may be enclosed various documents—the history of the church, and the building enterprise, copies of current newspapers, and anything else thought desirable—the box to be sealed up before it is deposited.

The place of the stone is in the main corner or angle of the foundation—the right-hand corner to one who stands facing the main entrance of the building —under the sill and water-table of the main floor of the edifice. Of course the foundations must be completed, including whatever of basement there may be, before the corner-stone can be laid.

The ceremony consists in putting the metallic box in its place, then laying the stone lid or cover upon the cavity, and with a trowel covering it with cement or mortar, and thus completely enclose and seal the box within the stone.

There are usually preparatory exercises, consisting of singing, reading the Scriptures, prayer, and one or more addresses appropriate to the occasion, by persons selected for the purpose.

Sometimes preceding the erection of a public building of special importance, the *breaking ground*—the removal of the first earth preparatory to laying the foundations—is made an occasion for some public services; mainly an address declarative of the purpose and importance of the structure to be erected.

DEDICATIONS.

THE dedication of a church edifice, when it is complete and ready for use, is supposed to be the solemnly setting it apart to its designed purpose, the worship of God, with appropriate religious services. The principal feature of the ceremony is usually a sermon by the pastor, or some other one chosen for the purpose.

Unfortunately, the raising of money to pay for the house has come to be an almost inevitable concomitant of dedications, pressed so persistently as well nigh to obliterate the religious character of the occasion.

It is by some contended that a house of worship should never be formally set apart and dedicated to the service of God, until it is entirely paid for; that the presentation to Almighty God of a house to his praise which is encumbered with debt, and on which creditors hold claims, is unbecoming and inconsistent. This view may be extreme, but it is better and safer than to dedicate houses with debts so heavy as to crush the energy and discourage the hope of the church.

CHURCH FINANCES.

THE growth of church life, and the success of church work, depend to a much larger extent than is generally supposed, on a wise and energetic management of church finances. Indeed the financial question is often the vital one. No amount of faith, or prayer, can make amends for a negligent or slovenly management of the business concerns of religion.

And yet there is a vast amount of non-management and mismanagement of finances among the churches. Many a church believes itself unable to sustain a pastor, that has abundant pecuniary ability for that purpose, if its business affairs were properly conducted. Many a church imposes on its pastor a burden of inconvenience and vexation which are as unjust as they are needless, because they do not pay his salary systematically and promptly, if indeed they pay it at all. They compel him to bear the reputation of carelessness, if not of dishonesty, because he cannot pay his own bills promptly, the church not paying him.

Such a shiftless habit of business is as discreditable to the church as it is annoying to the pastor, and cannot fail to give them an unenviable reputation in the community where they are located. And it is wholly without excuse. For a church, like an individual, however poor, can manage their affairs, however limited, in an energetic and systematic manner. But many business men, who conduct their own affairs prudently, seem destitute of all business capacity, when the secular concerns of the church are entrusted to them.

The following suggestions are worthy of serious consideration :

1. The best men for this work should be selected for it. It is not always easy to find men competent to the service. But the best men who can be secured should be appointed, and if possible induced to serve. Men who will manage wisely, safely, and with energy the trust committed to them.

2. Some system should be adopted, and followed. Nothing can be done well without system.

3. As to what the system shall be, must be left to those who work it. There are many good plans, though no one is equally good for all places, and for all sets of men to work. Get the best that can be devised under the circumstances.

4. After one system is faithfully tried, correct the faults which appear in the working of it, or adopt a better one, if a better one appears.

5. The weekly envelope plan of collections is now almost universally accepted as the best method of making collections. Small sums frequently collected are more easily secured, and more cheerfully given ; while the aggregates are large. This seems to have been the apostolic plan; a fact which gives it the stamp of divine approval.

6. Most churches prefer to retain the system of renting pews—at low prices—in connection with the envelope collections, rather than depend entirely on the envelopes, and adopt free seats. It gives a certain income from seat rents, allows a choice of pews at varied prices, and maintains the family-seat system in the house of worship.

7. No plan, however good, will work itself; while a poor plan, if judiciously and persistently prosecuted, will be largely successful. Therefore, whatever system be adopted, let it be in the hands of the best persons, and persistently followed up. Dealing with a slack hand will bring disaster anywhere.

8. No one has so vital an interest in the good financial management of the church, as the pastor; and no one can do so much to secure it, if he himself only have the prudence and the skill. As the pastor of the whole church, and all its departments of work, it is his privilege and duty to have the oversight of all, to counsel, advise, encourage, and stimulate, but not intrude into the sphere, nor needlessly interfere with the work of any others.

9. Let the pastor, however, beware attempting to manage the finances himself, or handle the funds of the church. If he does, he will almost inevitably be found fault with, charged with mistakes, mismanagement, and perhaps with malversation. Let him plan, advise, and stimulate, but put others forward to handle the money and be responsible for the business.

10. Frequent appeals to the congregation for money to make up deficiencies, have rather a depressing and unfortunate effect. All that can be done quietly

5

and privately, had better be so done. Yet the whole body should, at least once a year, know the condition of affairs, and respond to any appeal that may be made.

11. The true principle of collections is doubtless: 1. To get something from each individual, and if possible, in proportion to each one's ability. A few should not do all the giving. 2. Secure the contributions systematically. This will insure order, and form a habit of giving. 3. Make the collections frequently—at brief intervals. The sums will be smaller and more readily given. It will be more likely to make giving seem a Christian duty and privilege.

12. Depending on fairs, festivals, lectures, suppers, exhibitions and the like, to meet church expenses, is a mistaken and mischievous method of doing Christian work. The principle is wrong. Social entertainments, of a suitable character, and held under proper limitations, are commendable. They may sometimes, no doubt, be resorted to for revenue in specific cases. But if much used they demoralize Christian work, and dissipate if not destroy the spirituality of the church. Christians should give because it is their duty and privilege to give.

BENEVOLENT COLLECTIONS.

EVERY church should contribute statedly to the leading objects of Christian benevolence, which are sustained by the denomination. And yet a vast number of churches neglect this altogether. For this neglect, the pastor is largely responsible. Since, while many churches are quite indisposed, if not actually opposed to such contributions, the pastor can, if he will, in some way, secure a recognition of these objects, and a contribution for them, however small it may be. And if admitted to a hearing, and the form of support, they will grow in favor with the people.

The plea made by many feeble churches, that no appeal for aid must be made, except for themselves, is fallacious and harmful.

No church will ever grow stronger for refusing aid to all outside objects ; and no church will grow weaker for listening to the claims of others, or giving a little to aid worthy causes. Nor need a pastor fear that the giving to any worthy cause will prevent the payment of his salary. It will rather help, than hinder it.

1. It may not be wise for a church to attempt to sustain every good object that pleads for help. But they should select a few, deemed most deserving,

and which will be most likely to enlist the sympathies of the people. These perhaps would be, the Foreign Mission, Home Mission, Bible Cause, and State Convention, or Association Mission Work. These appeal directly and forcibly to every church, and should be allowed a hearing once a year. Other objects should, occasionally at least, be recognized.

2. Every church should have some system of benevolent work. The least troublesome way—but perhaps the least effective—is to have an agent come, present the cause, and take a collection. Better that than nothing.

3. A better plan, however, is for some convenient time to be fixed for each object, which the pastor himself shall present. An agent should not be waited for, nor depended on. If he can come and give them information, and stimulate their benevolence, it is very well; or spend his time where he is needed more. But the pastor should supervise it, and see that it is properly attended to.

4. Many churches depend on a mere plate collection. Some circulate cards, either to be used at the time, or taken home and returned with the names and amounts to be given; which amounts are to be collected afterwards. Some circulate small envelopes in which the contributors enclose their donations, and return them at some subsequent specified time, to be placed in the basket. In either case an efficient committee should have the matter in charge, and the pastor see that it is not neglected.

5. A more effective plan probably, is that of having a committee to take the whole matter in charge,

and solicit personally from each individual, a contri
bution for each of the objects aided; giving to each
its distinct and appropriate time; a presentation of
each object, to the congregation by the pastor, or
some other person, to precede each such specific
effort. This imposes somewhat more labor, but is
more successful in results.

6. Festivals, suppers, and exhibitions, properly
managed, may no doubt at times be safely used to
raise funds for benevolent objects. But to rely on
these largely, is to pervert the principle of doing good,
and to deprive donors of the blessing of giving to a
good cause, for the sake of doing good, and out of
love to Christ.

7. The pastor, as the leader of all church work,
should see to it that some plan be adopted, and carried out. But it is much better for him to see that
others do it, than to attempt to do it himself. What
work others can do, they should if possible perform;
while the pastor should expend his time and energy
on work which pertains to himself alone, and which
others cannot do.

8. The cultivation of systematic benevolence in a
church is the cultivation of true Christian character,
and tends to increase rather than diminish the liber-
ality with which its own expenses are met. For this
reason, if for no other, the pastor should encourage
and aid it. Those who never give, never wish to
give. Those who give from right motives, never
fail to find a blessing in it.

5*

TRUSTEES AND TEMPORALITIES.

THE pastor sustains an intimate relation to all departments of the church's life and work. As a leader, teacher, and overseer of the church, he is to be the counsellor, have the oversight, and seek the furtherance of all.

Trustees are appointed, and the rights of incorporation are obtained, for the purpose of holding the church property by a secure tenure, and managing its temporal concerns according to the provisions of law.

The following presents a brief and general view of church temporalities :

1. According to the laws of most States, trustees are elected—not by the church, as should be the case—but by a *society*, so called, composed of all persons of full age who worship there, and who contribute to the support of the worship.

2. The trustees are to have charge of the church's property, keep it in repair and good condition ; raise money for the current expenses, and pay out the same for bills due, including the pastor's salary ; all being done under the instructions of the *society* which elected them. But they cannot legally sell, encumber, nor alienate the property, close the house of worship against the church, change or withhold the pas-

tor's salary, without special instructions from the
society for so doing. They cannot tear down, enlarge
or build anew, nor purchase additional property,
without special instructions from the *society*.

They cannot legally fix, change, or interfere with
the times of worship, nor prevent the house from being used for religious purposes, according to the
wish of the church and its original design ; but can
prevent its being used for other than religious purposes. Nor can they themselves open the house for
any purpose at their own option, without the consent
of the church. They simply hold the property in
trust, for the church to use for its legitimate purposes.

3. The rights of the trustees for raising and expend-
ing funds, are confined strictly to the temporal con
cerns of the church. Funds for the more spiritual
affairs, as for the communion service, for the poor, for
missions, and other benevolent uses, they have nothing to do with. Those matters pertain strictly to
the deacons' office and work ; or they may be entrusted to special committees.

4. The pastor has no right of interference with the
trustees in their special sphere of service, but he
should keep well informed as to the business and
financial affairs of the church, counsel and advise,
encourage and aid them in their work. If trustees
were wise and prudent, they would constantly seek
the advice and co-operation of the pastor. But this
is seldom done.

5. It is not wise to have the financial affairs of the
church brought too frequently before the congrega-

tion, especially if it be to make up balances, or to repeat subscriptions, in order to rescue from desperate
emergencies. It makes a congregation restless, and
diverts thought too much from the more spiritual
purposes of worship. Such work should, for the
most part, be done quietly, and in private. But
when it becomes essential to bring it before the people, on the Sabbath, it should be done in harmony
with the sanctity of the place and the occasion, as a
matter of religion, and a part of worship itself.
For they who come into the presence of God with
"thanksgiving," should also bring an "offering" to
Him whom they worship.

6. It will be greatly wise on the pastor's part, to
avoid all personal collisions with the trustees. They
will doubtless at times differ in judgment as to matters of business, but these should be treated with
great caution and prudence. Many a pastor has
been driven from his church by the vexations which
trustees were able to impose upon him, directly or
indirectly. Finances embarrassed by intentional
complications, or equally intentional neglect, may
soon make the pastor's position unpleasant, if not
unendurable. He should be true to himself, and to
his office, even in the face of conduct so unjust and
dishonorable; but he should be very prudent. And
if prudent, he will seldom have trouble with his trustees.

SUNDAY-SCHOOL WORK.

SUNDAY-SCHOOLS have become an almost universally diffused means of religious culture, in
connection with church work and Christian activity.
The true relations of the school to the church and of
the pastor to the school, should be better understood
and more clearly defined than they seem to be. That
serious and more frequent difficulties do not arise in
connection with them, is due to the mutual good
sense, good feeling, and forbearance of Christian
workers engaged in church and school, rather than to
the want of occasion.

Suggestions, few and brief only, can be offered respecting the matter, in this place.

1. A church school should belong to the church.
It should be supported by, and under the control of
the church. While the church should not ordinarily
or needlessly interfere with its operations, it should
maintain the right to its general management. A
mission school holding no vital connection with the
church, and not sustained by it, cannot be controlled
by it.

2. The pastor, as pastor of the church and all its
work, is also pastor of the Sunday-school, its general
overseer and adviser. And the officers and teachers

stand in their own light, and are exceedingly un-wise, who do not often seek his counsel and co-opera-ation. But many Sunday-school workers seem purposely to stand aloof from, and almost if not quite in antagonism to both church and pastor.

3. The pastor should frequently visit the school, if but for a few minutes at a time, making such suggestions as he thinks are needed, and encouraging both teachers and pupils.

4. He should also, as far as possible, visit the parents of the pupils in their homes, and secure, if practicable, their attendance on the services of the church, in public worship.

5. It is not, however, wise, save in exceptional and pressing cases of necessity, for the pastor to become the acting superintendent of the school, admitting that he may be able to fill that office much better than any one else to be had. It imposes an amount of labor he ought not to perform; his ministerial and pastoral services are likely to deteriorate; and his relations to the people may become complicated and vexatious.

6. Nor is it wise for the pastor to become a teacher in the school. Many, especially young pastors, attempt this, but have to abandon the effort. All his thought, vigor, and energy should be given to his own appropriate ministerial work on the Sabbath. He would probably lose as much effectiveness from the pulpit, as he would furnish to the Sunday-school or the Bible Class.

7. But if he can have charge of a teachers' meeting or a Bible Class for the study of the Scriptures, some

time during the week, he will do an important and substantial service.

8. The pastor will materially further Sunday-school work, and perhaps correct mistaken ideas concerning it, by occasionally preaching on the subject.

9. One of the peculiar dangers to which this department of Christian work is exposed, is to superficial study, and to a superabundance of light and trifling entertainments. This is on the plea of interesting the children. But it easily invades the sphere of real religious work, and is liable to prevent rather than to further Bible study. It is the pastor's duty to watch the drift of things.

THE CHOIR, AND MUSIC.

STILL more intimately does the pastor stand rela
ted to the service of song, as a part of Christian
worship; and consequently to those who lead that
service. The people ought to sing the praises of God
in worship, and not permit that department of devotion to be performed wholly by a few selected singers.

Observation and experience extending over a
pretty wide field, have generally decided that congregational singing can be promoted better by the
use of a chorus choir to lead, than by either a quar-
tet or a precentor. A choir therefore, under ordinary circumstances, would constitute the best leader-
ship of song-worship in the church.

Singers are proverbially sensitive; stand a good
deal on the dignity of their position, and on their
capability, and are liable at times to become a little
factious. Churches have been not unfrequently agi-
tated, and sometimes thoroughly rent by choir troubles. Of course similar results have come to pass—
and perhaps quite as frequently—through trustees,
deacons, and even ministers themselves. So that
choirs should not have to bear undeserved blame.

1. As the pastor is the conductor of worship, the
services of the choir should be directly under his control. There cannot be two heads, two directing

wills, and of course two methods which may become diverse, and even antagonistic to each other, without difficulty resulting.

2. The pastor should use great discretion in his intercourse with the singers, avoid arbitrary dictation, encourage and commend them where it can be done, show an affectionate interest in them, and when they differ in opinion, take kindly counsel with them. A minister kind and wise will seldom have any serious difficulty with a choir.

3. Singers should, so far as practicable—and the leader always—be Christians. It would be as incongruous to appoint an unconverted man to lead the prayer meeting, as to lead the service of song for worship.

4. Volunteer choirs, recruited from the material which the church itself can furnish, are more in harmony with the genius of Christian worship, than hired singers engaged as mere performers would be. The true idea of singing in church, is, not that of a performance for the entertainment of an audience, but that of worship in song. And yet, if the leader, organist or others, devote to this service time and talent valuable to them, and have need, there is no reason why the church, if able, should not give them some compensation.

5. If practicable, every church should secure competent instruction in the elements of vocal music, during a part of the year—the winter months, for instance—for the benefit of the young particularly. This would very much further the purposes of congregational singing in church worship.

6. Praise meetings, so called, are now quite in vogue, as an attraction to religious service. If they can be made really praise meetings, and not a light social entertainment for the sake of drawing people together, they may become spiritually profitable, as well as attractive.

7. So great and so beneficent a power is sacred song, as a means of grace and an aid to devotion, that every pastor should labor, by all legitimate means, to promote its best uses and its highest culture in the church.

8. All that has been said as to the importance of singing in public service, applies with even more force to song in the social meetings for worship. Appropriate singing is almost the life of the prayer meeting. No effort should be spared to make it effective there.

THE PASTOR AND DEACONS.

THE design of the diaconate evidently was, not
that of a co-ordinate branch of church government, but a co-operative yet subordinate aid to the
ministerial and pastoral functions. The deacons are
to be helpers, counsellors and coadjutors to the pastor. Their special sphere of service is in the temporalities of the church; by attending to which matters
they relieve the pastor, and allow him to devote himself entirely to the ministry of the word, and to
spiritual concerns. They also become advisers and
helpers of the pastor in his work.

If the idea of the primitive church were carried
out, to the deacons would doubtless be committed the
department of secular church service now devolved
on trustees. But prevailing usage has narrowed
their sphere to the care of the poor and sick of the
church, serving at the communion, a sort of cabinet
council for the pastor, and a leading activity in the
general concerns of the church.

There is not unfrequently serious complaint against
deacons, that they occasion the pastor—and perhaps
the church too—much embarrassment and vexation,
by a desire for the pre-eminence, and an assumption
of official authority. No doubt this sometimes hap-
pens, as it will happen with persons who are not
deacons. But for the most part it is believed that

all difficulty can be avoided by a wise and prudent
course on the part of the pastor and the church, and
the diaconate be made to realize its original design,
and become a greatly helpful and beneficent service
in the furtherance of the gospel.

1. Great care should be used in the selection and
election of deacons, that none but suitable men be
put into office. This counsel cannot be too emphati-
cally urged. Men never should be elected to the
office, simply because there is a vacancy to be filled,
nor because they themselves or their friends desire
their election. Never, unless there is a service for
them to perform; never unless there are persons
whom the church, with some good degree of unanimity, believe to be fitted for the office; and never,
without much prayer for divine guidance in the selection. The church can get along better without
deacons, than with unfit deacons. To attempt to fill
sacred offices by partisan zeal and party caucusing,
is a scandal to the church and to religion.

2. If a man occupies the deacon's office who ob-
structs the church's work, and is a vexation and
hindrance rather than a help—and if, by frank and
faithful endeavor he cannot be brought into harmony
with the spirit of his office—he should by the church
be requested to resign. And if he will not resign,
after much patient and prayerful effort, it is the right
of the church, by vote, to declare his office vacant,
and in due time to fill his place with some one else.

3. For the harmony of the church, as well as for
his own comfort and usefulness, the pastor should
avoid all conflicts with his deacons. He has more a⁴

stake, if any question of prudence, propriety, or morality be raised, than they can have. Nor are conflicts necessary, except in very extreme cases.

4. On the contrary, if the pastor can have with him and supporting him a company of prudent, wise, and helpful deacons, it will give him great encouragement, and vast influence for good in his church. To secure this he should leave no proper means untried.

5. If the pastor can have his deacons meet with him, once a month, to look over the condition of the church, pray for its prosperity, and devise means for more effective work, it will ordinarily be of great advantage. Many difficulties can be privately and quietly corrected at their inception, and plans can be carefully matured before being presented to the body for its action.

6. But such meetings should not attempt to invade the prerogatives of the church, on any question of authority; nor to dispose of business which should come before the entire body. Nor would it be proper for the deacons to meet as a *board*, without the pastor's presence, and assume the right to act by themselves, as an independent official department in the church.

7. But any work specially committed to them by the church—as for instance the care of the poor—should not be needlessly interfered with by pastor or church. Yet both should be informed as to what they do, and the pastor should counsel and advise with them, as to the manner in which the work should be done.

6*

SELECTIONS

FROM THE

SACRED SCRIPTURES,

FOR USE ON

VARIOUS OCCASIONS,

OF

RELIGIOUS SERVICE,

BOTH

PUBLIC AND PRIVATE.

THANKSGIVING.

I.

PRAISE waiteth for thee, O God, in Zion: and unto thee shall the vow be performed. O thou that hearest prayer, unto thee shall all flesh come. Iniquities prevail against me; as for our transgressions, thou shalt purge them away. Blessed is the man whom thou choosest, and causest to approach unto thee, that he may dwell in thy courts: we shall be satisfied with the goodness of thy house, even of thy holy temple.—*Psalm* lxv. 1-4.

O clap your hands, all ye people; shout unto God with the voice of triumph. For the Lord most high is terrible; he is a great King over all the earth. He shall subdue the people under us, and the nations under our feet. He shall choose our inheritance for us, the excellency of Jacob whom he loved. God is gone up with a shout, the Lord with the sound of a trumpet. Sing praises to God, sing praises: sing praises unto our King, sing praises. For God is the king of all the earth: sing ye praises with understanding.—*Psalm* xlvii. 1–7.

Make a joyful noise unto God, all ye lands: Sing forth the honor of his name: make his praise glorious. Say unto God, How terrible art thou in thy works! through the greatness of thy power shall thine enemies submit themselves unto thee. All the earth shall worship thee, and shall sing unto thee; they shall sing to thy name.—*Psalm* lxvi. 1–4.

O Lord our Lord, how excellent is thy name in all the earth! who hast set thy glory above the heavens. Out of the mouth of babes and sucklings hast thou ordained strength because of thine enemies, that thou mightest still the enemy and the avenger. When I consider thy heavens, the work of thy fingers; the moon and the stars, which thou hast ordained; what is man, that thou art mindful of him? and the son of man, that thou visitest him?—*Psalm* viii. 1–4.

O come, let us sing unto the Lord: let us make a joyful noise to the rock of our salvation. Let us come before his presence with thanksgiving, and make a joyful noise unto him with psalms. For the Lord is a great God, and a great King above all gods. In his hand are the deep places of the earth: the strength of the hills is his also. The sea is his, and he made it: and his hands formed the dry land. O come, let us

worship and bow down: let us kneel before the
Lord our maker: For he is our God, and we are
the people of his pasture, and the sheep of his
hand.—*Psalm* xcv. 1–7.

II.

O sing unto the Lord a new song: sing unto
the Lord, all the earth. Sing unto the Lord,
bless his name; shew forth his salvation from
day to day. Declare his glory among the heathen, his wonders among all people. For the
Lord is great, and greatly to be praised: he is
to be feared above all gods. For all the gods
of the nations are idols: but the Lord made the
heavens. Honor and majesty are before him:
strength and beauty are in his sanctuary. Give
unto the Lord, O ye kindreds of the people, give
unto the Lord, glory and strength. Give unto
the Lord the glory due unto his name: bring an
offering, and come into his courts.

O worship the Lord in the beauty of holiness: fear before him, all the earth. Say among
the heathen that the Lord reigneth; the world
also shall be established that it shall not be
moved: he shall judge the people righteously.
Let the heavens rejoice, and let the earth be
glad; let the sea roar, and the fullness thereof.
Let the field be joyful, and all that is therein:
then shall all the trees of the wood rejoice be-

fore the Lord ; for he cometh, for he cometh to
judge the earth : he shall judge the world with
righteousness, and the people with his truth.—
Psalm xcvi. 1–13.

O God, my heart is fixed; I will sing and
give praise, even with my glory. Awake, psal-
tery and harp : I myself will awake early. I
will praise thee, O Lord, among the people:
and I will sing praises unto thee among the
nations. For thy mercy is great above the heavens : and thy truth reacheth unto the clouds.
Be thou exalted, O God, above the heavens :
and thy glory 'above all the earth; That thy
beloved may be delivered : save with thy right
hand, and answer me.—*Psalm* cviii. 1–6.

Let the people praise thee, O God; let all
the people praise thee. O let the nations be
glad and sing for joy : for thou shalt judge the
people righteously, and govern the nations upon
earth. Let the people praise thee, O God; let
all the people praise thee. Then shall the
earth yield her increase; and God, even our
own God, shall bless us. God shall bless us ;
and all the ends of the earth shall fear him.—
Psalm lxvii. 3–7.

I will praise thee with my whole heart : before the gods will l sing praise unto thee. I will
worship toward thy holy temple, and praise thy
name for thy lovingkindness and for thy truth:

for thou hast magnified thy word above all thy name. In the day when I cried, thou answeredst me, and strengthenedst me with strength in my soul. All the kings of the earth shall praise thee, O Lord, when they hear the words of thy mouth. Yea, they shall sing in the ways of the Lord; for great is the glory of the Lord.

Though the Lord be high, yet hath he respect unto the lowly: but the proud he knoweth afar off. Though I walk in the midst of trouble, thou wilt revive me: thou shalt stretch forth thy hand against the wrath of my enemies, and thy right hand shall save me. The Lord will perfect that which concerneth me: thy mercy, O Lord, endureth forever: forsake not the works of thine own hands.—*Psalm* cxxxviii. 1–8.

I will extol thee, my God, O King; and I will bless thy name for ever and ever. Every day will I bless thee; and I will praise thy name for ever and ever. Great is the Lord, and greatly to be praised; and his greatness is unsearchable. One generation shall praise thy works to another, and shall declare thy mighty acts. I will speak of the glorious honor of thy majesty, and of thy wondrous works. And men shall speak of the might of thy terrible act; and I will declare thy greatness.—*Psalm* cxlv. 1–6.

7

III.

O sing unto the Lord a new song; **for he**
hath done marvelous things : his right hand, and
his holy arm, hath gotten him the victory. The
Lord hath made known his salvation : his righteousness hath he openly showed in the sight of
the heathen. He hath remembered his mercy
and his truth toward the house of Israel : all
the ends of the earth have seen the salvation
of our God. Make a joyful noise unto the
Lord, all the earth : make a loud noise, and rejoice, and sing praise.

Sing unto the Lord with the harp; with
the harp, and the voice of a psalm. With
trumpets and sound of cornet make a joyful
noise before the Lord, the King. Let the sea
roar, and the fullness thereof; the world, and
they that dwell therein. Let the floods clap
their hands : let the hills be joyful together
before the Lord; for he cometh to judge
the earth : with righteousness shall he judge
the world, and the people with equity.—*Psalm*
xcviii. 1–9.

Praise ye the Lord. Sing unto the Lord a
new song and his praise in the congregation of
saints. Let Israel rejoice in him that **made**
him : let the children of Zion be joyful in their
King. Let them praise his name in the **dance:**

let them sing praises unto him with the timbrel and harp. For the Lord taketh pleasure in his people, he will beautify the meek with salvation. Let the saints be joyful in glory: let them sing aloud upon their beds. Let the high praises of God be in their mouth, and a two-edged sword in their hand.—*Psalm* cxlix. 1-6.

The Lord liveth; and blessed be my rock; and exalted be the God of the rock of my salvation. It is God that avengeth me, and that bringeth down the people under me, and that bringeth me forth from my enemies: thou also hast lifted me up on high above them that rose up against me: thou hast delivered me from the violent man. Therefore I will give thanks unto thee, O Lord, among the heathen, and I will sing praises unto thy name. He is the tower of salvation for his king: and showeth mercy to his anointed, unto David, and to his seed for evermore.—2 *Sam.* xxii. 47-51.

Sing unto the Lord a new song, and his praise from the end of the earth, ye that go down to the sea, and all that is therein; the isles, and the inhabitants thereof. Let the wilderness and the cities thereof lift up their voice, the villages that Kedar doth inhabit: let the inhabitants of the rock sing, let them shout from the top of the mountains. Let them give glory unto the Lord, and declare his praise in the islands.—*Isa.* xlii. 10-12.

Praise ye the Lord: for it is good to sing praises unto our God; for it is pleasant, and praise is comely. The Lord doth build up Jerusalem: he gathereth together the outcasts of Israel. He healeth the broken in heart, and bindeth up their wounds.—*Psalm* cxlvii. 1–3.

And after these things I heard a great voice of much people in heaven, saying, Alleluia: Salvation, and glory, and honor and power, unto the Lord our God.—*Rev.* xix. 1.

Unto him that loved us, and washed us from our sins in his own blood, and hath made us kings and priests unto God and his Father; to him be glory and dominion for ever and ever. Amen.—*Rev.* i. 5, 6.

FASTING.

I.

BLOW the trumpet in Zion, sanctify a fast, call a solemn assembly : gather the people, sanctify the congregation, assemble the elders, gather the children, and those that suck the breasts : let the bridegroom go forth of his chamber, and the bride out of her closet. Let the priests, the ministers of the Lord, weep between the porch and the altar, and let them say, Spare thy people, O Lord, and give not thy heritage to reproach, that the heathen should rule over them : wherefore should they say among the people, Where is their God ?—*Joel* ii. 15–17.

Therefore also now, saith the Lord, turn ye even to me with all your heart, and with fasting, and with weeping, and with mourning : And rend your heart, and not your garments, and turn unto the Lord your God : for he is gracious and merciful, slow to anger, and of great kindness, and repenteth him of the evil. Who knoweth if he will return and repent, and leave a blessing behind him ; even a meat-offering and a drink-offering unto the Lord your God ?—*Joel* ii. 12–14.

7*

Wherefore have we fasted, say they, and thou
seest not? wherefore have we afflicted our soul,
and thou takest no knowledge? Behold, in the
day of your fast ye find pleasure, and exact all
your labors. Behold, ye fast for strife and debate, and to smite with the fist of wickedness:
ye shall not fast as ye do this day, to make your
voice to be heard on high.

Is it such a fast that I have chosen? a day for
a man to afflict his soul? is it to bow down his
head as a bulrush, and to spread sackcloth and
ashes under him? wilt thou call this a fast, and
an acceptable day to the Lord? Is not this the
fast that I have chosen—to loose the bands of
wickedness, to undo the heavy burdens, and to
let the oppressed go free, and that ye break
every yoke? Is it not to deal thy bread to the
hungry, and that thou bring the poor that are
cast out to thy house? when thou seest the naked, that thou cover him; and that thou hide
not thyself from thy own flesh?

Then shall thy light break forth as the morning, and thy health shall spring forth speedily:
and thy righteousness shall go before thee; the
glory of the Lord shall be thy reward. Then
shalt thou call, and the Lord shall answer; thou
shalt cry, and he shalt say, Here I am. If thou
take away from the midst of thee the yoke, the
putting forth of the finger, and speaking vanity;

and if thou draw out thy soul to the hungry, and
satisfy the afflicted soul ; then shall thy light
rise in obscurity, and thy darkness be as the
noonday : and the Lord shall guide thee continually, and satisfy thy soul in drought, and make
fat thy bones : and thou shalt be like a watered
garden, and like a spring of water, whose waters
fail not.—*Isa.* lviii. 3–11.

II.

Sanctify ye a fast : call a solemn assembly :
gather the elders, and all the inhabitants of the
land into the house of the Lord your God, and
cry unto the Lord.—*Joel* i. 14.

So the people of Nineveh believed God, and
proclaimed a fast, and put on sackcloth, from
the greatest of them even to the least of them.
For word came unto the king of Nineveh, and
he arose from his throne, and he laid his robe
from him, and covered him with sackcloth, and
sat in ashes. And he caused it to be proclaimed
and published through Nineveh by the decree
of the king and his nobles, saying, Let neither
man nor beast, herd nor flock, taste any thing :
let them not feed, nor drink water : but let man
and beast be covered with sackcloth, and cry
mightily unto God : yea, let them turn every
one from his evil way, and from the violence
that is in their hands Who can tell if God will

turn and repent, and turn away from his fierce
anger, that we perish not?

And God saw their works, that they turned
from their evil way; and God repented of the
evil that he had said that he would do unto
them; and he did it not.—*Jonah* iii. 5–10.

Moreover, when ye fast, be not as the hypocrites, of a sad countenance: for they disfigure
their faces, that they may appear unto men to
fast. Verily I say unto you, they have their reward. But thou, when thou fastest, anoint thy
head, and wash thy face; that thou appear not
unto men to fast, but unto thy Father which is
in secret: and thy Father which seeth in secret,
shall reward thee openly.—*Matt.* vi. 16–18.

And the disciples of John and of the Pharisees
used to fast: and they come and say unto him,
Why do the disciples of John and of the Pharisees fast, but thy disciples fast not? And Jesus
said unto them, Can the children of the bride-
chamber fast, while the bridegroom is with them?
as long as they have the bridegroom with them,
they cannot fast. But the days will come, when
the bridegroom shall be taken away from them,
and then shall they fast in those days.—*Mark*
ii. 18–20.

CONFESSION.

I.

BEHOLD, I am vile; what shall I answer thee? I will lay my hand upon my mouth. Once have I spoken; but I will not answer: yea twice; but I will proceed no further.—*Job* xl. 4, 5

I have sinned; what shall I do unto thee, O thou Preserver of men? why hast thou set me as a mark against thee, so that I am a burden to myself? And why dost thou not pardon my transgression, and take away my iniquity? for now shall I sleep in the dust; and thou shalt seek me in the morning, but I shall not be.—*Job* vii. 20, 21.

For our transgressions are multiplied before thee, and our sins testify against us: for our transgressions are with us; and as for our iniquities, we know them; In transgressing and lying against the Lord, and departing away from our God, speaking oppression and revolt, conceiving and uttering from the heart words of falsehood. And judgment is turned away backward, and justice standeth afar off: for truth is fallen in the street, and equity cannot enter.

Yea, truth faileth; and he that departeth **from**
evil maketh himself a prey.—*Isa.* lix. 12–15.

For innumerable evils have compassed **me**
about: my iniquities have taken hold upon me,
so that I am not able to look up; they are more
than the hairs of my head: therefore my heart
faileth me. Be pleased, O Lord, to deliver me:
O Lord, make haste to help me.—*Psalm* xl. 12,
13.

I fell upon my knees, and spread out my hands
unto the Lord my God, and said, O my God, I
am ashamed and blush to lift up my face to thee,
my God; for our iniquities are increased over
our head and our trespass is grown up unto the
heavens.—*Ezra* ix. 5, 6.

I beseech thee, O Lord God of heaven, the
great and terrible God, that keepeth covenant
and mercy for them that love him and observe
his commandments: let thy ear now be attentive,
and thy eyes open, that thou mayest hear the
prayer of thy servant, which I pray before thee
now, day and night, for the children of Israel
thy servants, and confess the sins of the children of Israel, which we have sinned against thee:
both I and my father's house have sinned. We
have dealt very corruptly against thee, and have
not kept the commandments, nor the statutes,
nor the judgments, which thou commandest thy
servant Moses.—*Neh.* i. 5–7.

II.

Have mercy upon me, O God, according to thy lovingkindness: according unto the multitude of thy tender mercies blot out my transgressions. For I acknowledge my transgressions: and my sin is ever before me. Against thee, thee only, have I sinned, and done this evil in thy sight: that thou mightest be justified when thou speakest, and be clear when thou judgest.—*Psalm* li. 1, 3, 4.

We have sinned, and have committed iniquity, and have done wickedly, and have rebelled, even by departing from thy precepts and from thy judgments: neither have we hearkened unto thy servants the prophets, which spake in thy name to our kings, our princes, and our fathers, and to all the people of the land. O Lord, righteousness belongeth unto thee, but unto us confusion of faces, as at this day; to the men of Judah, and to the inhabitants of Jerusalem, and unto all Israel, that are near, and that are afar off, through all the countries thou hast driven them, because of their trespass that they have trespassed against thee.

O Lord, to us belongeth confusion of face, to our kings, to our princes, and to our fathers, because we have sinned against thee. To the **Lord our God** belong mercies and forgivenesses, though we have rebelled against him; neither have we obeyed the voice of the Lord our God, to walk in his laws, which he set before us by his servants the prophets.—*Dan.* ix. 5–10.

O Lord, though our iniquities testify against us, do thou it for thy name's sake: for our backslidings are many; we have sinned against thee.—*Jer.* xiv. 7

O Lord, hear; O Lord, forgive; O Lord, hearken and do; defer not, for thy own sake, O my God: for thy city and thy people are called by thy name.—*Dan.* ix. 19.

SUPPLICATION.

I.

HEAR my prayer, O Lord, give ear to my supplications: in thy faithfulness answer me, and in thy righteousness. And enter not into judgment with thy servant: for in thy sight shall no man living be justified. For the enemy hath persecuted my soul; he hath smitten my life down to the ground; he hath made me to dwell in darkness, as those that have been long dead. Therefore is my spirit overwhelmed within me: my heart within me is desolate.

I remember the days of old; I meditate on all thy works; I muse on the work of thy hands. I stretch forth my hands unto thee: my soul thirsteth after thee, as a thirsty land. Selah. Hear me speedily, O Lord; my spirit faileth; hide not thy face from me, lest I be like unto them that go down into the pit. Cause me to hear thy lovingkindness in the morning; for in thee do I trust; cause me to know the way wherein I should walk; for I lift up my soul unto thee.—*Psalm* cxliii. 1–8.

But as for me, my prayer is unto thee, O
Lord, in an acceptable time: O God, in the
multitude of thy mercy hear me, in the truth
of thy salvation. Deliver me out of the mire,
and let me not sink: let me be delivered from
them that hate me, and out of the deep waters.
Let not the waterflood overflow me, neither let
the deep swallow me up, and let not the pit
shut her mouth upon me. Hear me, O Lord;
for thy lovingkindness is good: turn unto me
according to the multitude of thy tender mercies. And hide not thy face from thy servant;
for I am in trouble: hear me speedily. Draw
nigh unto my soul and redeem it : deliver me
because of my enemies.—*Psalm* lxix. 13–18.

And said, I beseech thee, O Lord God of
heaven, the great and terrible God, that keepeth
covenant and mercy for them that love him and
observe his commandments : Let thy ear be
now attentive, and thy eyes open, that thou
mayest hear the prayer of thy servant, which
I pray before thee now, day and night, for the
children of Israel thy servants, and confess the
sins of the children of Israel, which we have
sinned against thee : both I and my father's
house have sinned. O Lord, I beseech thee, let
now thy ear be attentive to the prayer of thy
servant, and to the prayer of thy servants, who
desire to fear thy name ; and prosper, I pray

thee, thy servant this day, and grant him mercy
in the sight of this man.—*Neh.* i. 5, 6, 11.

II.

O Lord God of my salvation, I have cried day
and night before thee : let my prayer come before thee : incline thine ear unto my cry ; for
my soul is full of troubles : and my life draweth
nigh unto the grave.—*Psalm* lxxxviii. 1–3.

Unto thee, O Lord, do I lift up my soul. O
my God, I trust in thee : let me not be ashamed,
let not my enemies triumph over me. Yea, let
none that wait on thee be ashamed : let them
be ashamed which transgress without cause.
Show me thy ways, O Lord; teach me thy
paths. Lead me in thy truth, and teach me ;
for thou art the God of my salvation : on thee do
I wait all the day. Remember, O Lord, thy
tender mercies and thy lovingkindnesses ; for
they have been ever of old. Remember not the
sins of my youth, nor my transgressions : according to thy mercy remember thou me for
thy goodness' sake, O Lord.—*Psalm* xxv. 1–7.

Have mercy upon me, O God, according to
thy lovingkindness : according unto the multitude of thy tender mercies blot out my transgressions. Wash me thoroughly from mine
iniquity, and cleanse me from my sin. Hide thy
face from my sins, and blot out all my iniquities.

Create in me a clean heart, O God ; and renew a right spirit within me. Cast me not away from thy presence ; and take not the Holy Spirit from me. Restore unto me the joy of thy salvation ; and uphold me with thy free Spirit. Then will I teach transgressors thy ways ; and sinners shall be converted unto thee.—*Psalm* li. 1–3, 9–13.

Teach me, O Lord, the way of thy statutes ; and I shall keep it unto the end. Give me understanding, and I shall keep thy law ; yea, I shall observe it with my whole heart. Make me to go in the path of thy commandments ; for therein do I delight. Incline my heart unto thy testimonies, and not to covetousness. Turn away my eyes from beholding vanity ; and quicken thou me in thy way. Establish thy word unto thy servant, who is devoted to thy fear. Turn away my reproach which I fear : for thy judgments are good. Behold, I have longed after thy precepts : quicken me in thy righteousness.—*Psalm* cxix. 33–40.

MINISTERS.*

I.

HOW beautiful upon the mountains are the feet of him that bringeth good tidings, that publisheth peace; that bringeth good tidings of good, that publisheth salvation; that saith unto Zion, thy God reigneth! Thy watchman shall lift up the voice; with the voice together shall they sing: for they shall see eye to eye, when the Lord shall bring again Zion.— *Isa.* lii. 7, 8.

How then shall they call on him in whom they have not believed? and how shall they believe in him of whom they have not heard? and how shall they hear without a preacher? and how shall they preach except they be sent? As it is written, how beautiful are the feet of them that preach the gospel of peace, and bring glad tidings of good things!—*Rom.* x. 14, 16.

And he gave some, apostles; and some, prophets; and some, evangelists; and some, pastors

---

* This section will be appropriate to the ordination, designation, or installation of ministers.

8*

and teachers ; for the perfecting of the saints,
for the work of the ministry, for the edifying of
the body of Christ : till we all come in the uni-
ty of the faith, and of the knowledge of the Son
of God, unto a perfect man, unto the measure
of the statute of the fullness of Christ.—*Eph.* iv.
11–13.

After these things, the Lord appointed other
seventy also, and sent them two and two before
his face, into every city and place, whither he
himself would come. Therefore said he unto
them, The harvest truly is great, but the laborers are few : pray ye therefore the Lord of the
harvest, that he would send forth laborers into
his harvest. Go your ways : behold, I send
you forth as lambs among wolves. Carry neither purse, nor scrip, nor shoes : and salute no
man by the way.

And into whatsoever house ye enter, first say,
Peace be to this house. And if the son of
peace be there, your peace shall rest upon it;
if not, it shall turn to you again. And in the
same house remain, eating and drinking such
things as they give; for the laborer is worthy
of his hire. Go not from house to house. And
into whatsoever city ye enter, and they receive
you, eat such things as are set before you. And
heal the sick that are therein, and say unto them,
The kingdom of God is come nigh unto you.

But into whatsoever city ye enter, and they receive you not, go your ways out into the streets of the same, and say, Even the very dust of your city, which cleaveth on us, we do wipe off against you: notwithstanding, be ye sure of this, that the kingdom of God is come nigh unto you. But I say unto you, That it shall be more tolerable in that day for Sodom, than for that city.

Wo unto thee, Chorazin! wo unto thee, Bethsaida! for if the mighty works had been done in Tyre and Sidon, which hath been done in you, they had a great while ago repented, sitting in sackcloth and ashes. But it shall be more tolerable for Tyre and Sidon at the judgment than for you. And thou, Capernaum, which art exalted to heaven, shalt be thrust down to hell. He that heareth you, heareth me; and he that despiseth you, despiseth me; and he that despiseth me, despiseth him that sent me.

And the seventy returned again with joy, saying, Lord, even the devils are subject unto us through thy name. And he said unto them, I beheld Satan as lightning fall from heaven. Behold, I give unto you power to tread on serpents and scorpions, and over all the power of the enemy: and nothing shall by any means hurt you. Notwithstanding, in this rejoice not, that the spirits are subject unto you; but rather rejoice,

because your names are written in heaven.—
Luke x. 1–20.

Then said Jesus to them again, peace be unto you : as my Father hath sent me, even so send
I you. And when he had said this, he breathed
on them, and saith unto them, Receive ye the
Holy Spirit.—*John* xx. 21, 22.

Jesus saith to Simon Peter, Simon, son of
Jonas, lovest thou me more than these? He
saith unto him, Yea, Lord ; thou knowest that I
love thee. He saith unto him, Feed my lambs.
He saith to him again the second time, Simon, son
of Jonas, lovest thou me? He saith unto him,
Yea, Lord ; thou knowest that I love thee. He
saith unto him, Feed my sheep. He saith unto
him the third time, Simon, son of Jonas, lovest
thou me? Peter was grieved because he said
unto him the third time, Lovest thou me? And
he said unto him, Lord, thou knowest all things;
thou knowest that I love thee. Jesus saith unto him, Feed my sheep.—*John* xxi. 15–17.

II.

And Jesus went about all the cities and villages, teaching in their synagogues, and preaching the gospel of the kingdom, and healing every sickness and every disease among the people. But when he saw the multitudes, he was
moved with compassion on them, because they

fainted, and were scattered abroad, as sheep having no shepherd. Then saith he unto his disciples, The harvest truly is plenteous, but the laborers are few; pray ye therefore the Lord of the harvest, that he will send forth laborers into his harvest.—*Matt.* ix. 35–38.

And he called unto him the twelve, and began to send them forth by two and two; and gave them power over unclean spirits; and commanded them that they should take nothing for their journey, save a staff only; no scrip, no bread, no money in their purse: but be shod with sandals; and not put on two coats. And he said unto them, In what place soever ye enter into an house, there abide till ye depart from that place.—*Mark* vi. 7–10.

He that receiveth you, receiveth me; and he that receiveth me, receiveth him that sent me. He that receiveth a prophet in the name of a prophet, shall receive a prophet's reward; and he that receiveth a righteous man in the name of a righteous man, shall receive a righteous man's reward. And whosoever shall give to drink unto one of these little ones, a cup of cold water only, in the name of a disciple, verily, I say unto you, he shall in no wise lose his reward.—*Matt.* x. 40–42.

And whosoever shall not receive you, nor hear you, when ye depart thence, shake off the dust under your feet, for a testimony against them. Verily, I say unto you, It shall be more tolerable for Sodom and Gomorrah in the day of judgment, than for that city. And they went out, and preached that men should repent.—*Mark* vi. 11, 12.

If a man desire the office of a bishop, he desireth a good work. A bishop must then be blameless, the husband of one wife, vigilant, sober, of good behavior, given to hospitality, apt to teach; not given to wine, no striker, not greedy of filthy lucre; but patient, not a brawler, not covetous; one that ruleth well his own house, having his children in subjection with all gravity; For if a man know not how to rule his own house, how shall he take care of the church of God? Not a novice, lest being lifted up with pride he fall into the condemnation of the devil. Moreover, he must have a good report of them which are without; lest he fall into reproach and the snare of the devil.—1 *Tim.* iii. 1–7.

III.

Thou therefore, my son, be strong in the grace that is in Christ Jesus. And the things that thou hast heard of me among many witnesses, the same commit thou to faithful men, who shall be able to teach others also. Thou, therefore, endure hardness, as a good soldier of Jesus Christ. No man that warreth entangleth himself with the affairs of this life; that he may please him who hath chosen him to be a soldier. And if a man also strive for masteries, yet is he not crowned, except he strive lawfully. Of these things, put them in remembrance, charging them before the Lord, that they strive not about words to no profit, but to the subverting of the hearers.

Study to show thyself approved unto God, a workman that needeth not to be ashamed, rightly dividing the word of truth. But shun profane and vain babblings; for they will increase unto more ungodliness. Flee also youthful lusts; but follow righteousness, faith, charity, peace, with them that call on the Lord out of a pure heart. But foolish and unlearned questions avoid, knowing that they do gender strifes. And the servant of the Lord must not strive; but be gentle unto all men, apt to teach, patient, in meekness instructing those that oppose themselves; if God peradventure will give them repentance to the acknowledging of the truth; and that they may recover themselves out of the snare of the devil, who are taken captive by him at his will.—2 *Tim.* ii. 1–5, 14–16, 22–26.

But continue thou in the things which thou

hast learned and hast been assured of, **knowing**
of whom thou hast learned them; and that from
a child thou hast known the holy scriptures,
which are able to make thee wise unto salvation
through faith which is in Christ Jesus. All
scripture is given by inspiration of God, and is
profitable for doctrine, for reproof, for correction,
for instruction in righteousness: That the man
of God may be perfect, thoroughly furnished
unto all good works.—2 *Tim*. iii. 14–17.

But speak thou the things which become
sound doctrine: In all things showing **thyself**
a pattern of good works: in doctrine showing
uncorruptness, gravity, sincerity, sound speech,
that cannot be condemned; that he that is of,
the contrary part may be ashamed, having no
evil thing to say of you. For the grace of **God**
that bringeth salvation hath appeared to all **men**,
teaching us that, denying ungodliness and worldly lusts, we should live soberly, righteously, **and**
godly, in this present world; Looking for **that**
blessed hope, and the glorious appearing of **the**
great God and our Saviour Jesus Christ; **who**
gave himself for us, that he might redeem **us**
from all iniquity, and purify unto him elf **a**
peculiar people, zealous of good works. **These**
things speak, and exhort, and rebuke with **all**
authority. Let no man despise thee.—***Titus*** **ii.**
1–8, 11–15.

Giving no offence in any thing, that the min·
istry be not blamed : but in all things approving
ourselves as the ministers of God.—2 *Cor.* vi. 3–4.

Therefore, seeing we have this ministry, as we
have received mercy, we faint not; but have
renounced the hidden things of dishonesty, not
walking in craftiness, nor handling the word of
God deceitfully; but by manifestation of the
truth, commending ourselves to every man's
conscience in the sight of God. For we preach
not ourselves, but Christ Jesus the Lord; and
ourselves your servants for Jesus' sake.—2 *Cor.*
iv. 1, 2, 5.

IV.

I charge thee therefore before God, and the
Lord Jesus Christ, who shall judge the quick
and the dead at his appearing and his kingdom,
preach the word; be instant in season, out of
season; reprove, rebuke, exhort with all long-
suffering and doctrine. For the time will come
when they will not endure sound doctrine; but
after their own lusts shall they heap to them·
selves teachers, having itching ears; and they
shall turn away their ears from the truth, and
shall be turned unto fables. But watch thou in
all things, endure affliction, do the work of an
evangelist, make full proof of thy ministry.—2
Tim. iv. 1–5.

9

Ordain elders in every city, as I had appointed thee: if any be blameless, the husband of one wife, having faithful children not accused of riot or unruly. For a bishop must be blameless, as the steward of God; not selfwilled, not soon angry, not given to wine, no striker, not given to filthy lucre; but a lover of hospitality, a lover of good men, sober, just, holy, temperate; holding fast the faithful word as he hath been taught, that he may be able by sound doctrine both to exhort and convince the gainsayers.— *Titus* i. 5–9.

Rebuke not an elder, but entreat him as a father; and the younger men as brethren. Let the elders that rule well be counted worthy of double honor, especially they who labor in the word and doctrine. For the scripture saith, Thou shalt not muzzle the ox that treadeth out the corn. And, The laborer is worthy of his reward. Against an elder receive not an accusation, but before two or three witnesses. Them that sin rebuke before all, that others also may fear. I charge thee before God, and the Lord Jesus Christ, and the elect angels, that thou observe these things without preferring one before another, doing nothing by partiality. Lay hands suddenly on no man, neither be partaker of other men's sins: keep thyself pure.—1 *Tim.* v. 1, 2, 17–22.

Fight the good fight of faith, lay hold on eternal life, whereunto thou art also called, and hast professed a good profession before many witnesses. I give thee charge in the sight of God, who quickeneth all things, and before Christ Jesus, who before Pontius Pilate witnessed a good confession: that thou keep this commandment without spot, unrebukable, until the appearing of our Lord Jesus Christ: which in his times he shall shew, who is the blessed and only Potentate, the King of kings, and Lord of lords: who only hath immortality, dwelling in the light which no man can approach unto; whom no man hath seen, nor can see; to whom be honor and power everlasting. Amen.

Charge them that are rich in this world, that they be not high-minded, nor trust in uncertain riches, but in the living God, who giveth us richly all things to enjoy: that they do good, that they be rich in good works, ready to distribute, willing to communicate: laying up in store for themselves a good foundation against the time to come, that they may lay hold on eternal life. O Timothy, keep that which is committed to thy trust, avoiding profane and vain babblings, and oppositions of science, falsely so called: which some professing, have erred concerning the faith. Grace be with thee. Amen.—1 *Tim.* vi. 12–21.

V.

Son of man, I have made thee a watchman
unto the house of Israel: therefore hear the word
at my mouth, and give them warning from me.
When I say unto the wicked, Thou shalt surely
die ; and thou givest him not warning, nor speakest to warn the wicked from his wicked way, to
save his life ; the same wicked man shall die in
his iniquity ; but his blood will I require at thy
hand.   Yet if thou warn the wicked, and he turn
not from his wickedness, nor from his wicked
way, he shall die in his iniquity ; but thou hast
delivered thy soul.

Again, When a righteous man doth turn from
his righteousness, and commit iniquity, and I
lay a stumbling block before him, he shall die:
because thou hast not given him warning, he
shall die in his sin, and his righteousness which
he hath done shall not be remembered ; but his
blood will I require at thy hand.   Nevertheless,
if thou warn the righteous man, that the righteous sin not, and he doth not sin, he shall surely
live, because he is warned; also thou hast delivered thy soul.—*Ezek.* iii. 17–21.

As every man hath received the gift, even so
minister the same one to another, as good stew-
ards of the manifold grace of God.   If any man
speak, let him speak as the oracles of God ; if

any man minister, let him do it as of the ability which God giveth: that God in all things may be glorified through Jesus Christ, to whom be praise and dominion for ever and ever.— 1 *Pet.* iv. 10, 11.

Study to show thyself approved unto God, a workman that needeth not be ashamed, rightfully dividing the word of truth. But shun profane and vain babblings; for they will increase unto more ungodliness.—2 *Tim.* ii. 15, 16.

O son of man, I have set thee a watchman unto the house of Israel; therefore thou shalt hear the word at my mouth, and warn them from me. When I say unto the wicked, O wicked man, thou shalt surely die: if thou dost not speak to warn the wicked from his way, that wicked man shall die in his iniquity, but his blood will I require at thy hand. Nevertheless, if thou warn the wicked of his way to turn from it; if he do not turn from his way, he shall die in his iniquity; but thou hast delivered thy soul. —*Ezek.* xxxiii. 7–9.

If thou put the brethren in remembrance of these things, thou shalt be a good minister of Jesus Christ, nourished up in the words of faith and of good doctrine, whereunto thou hast attained. These things command and teach. Let no man despise thy youth; but be thou an example of the believers, in word,

9*

in conversation, in charity, in spirit, in faith, in purity. Till I come, give attendance to reading, to exhortation, to doctrine.

Neglect not the gift that is in thee, which was given thee by prophecy, with the laying on of the hands of the presbytery. Meditate on these things; give thyself wholly to them: that thy profiting may appear unto all. Take heed unto thyself, and unto the doctrine : continue in them : for in doing this, thou shalt both save thyself, and them that hear thee.—1 *Tim.* iv. 6, 11–16.

Feed the flock of God which is among you, taking the oversight thereof, not by constraint, but willingly: not for filthy lucre, but of a ready mind ; neither as being lords over God's heritage, but being ensamples to the flock. And when the chief Shepherd shall appear, ye shall receive a crown of glory that fadeth not away.—1 *Pet.* v. 2–4.

Go ye into all the world, and preach the gospel to every creature. He that believeth, and is baptized, shall be saved ; but he that believeth not shall be damned.—*John* xvi. 15, 16.

DEACONS.

AND in those days, when the number of the disciples was multiplied, there arose a murmuring of the Grecians against the Hebrews, because their widows were neglected in the daily ministration. Then the twelve called the multitude of the disciples unto them, and said, It is not reason that we should leave the word of God, and serve tables. Wherefore, brethren, look ye out among you seven men of honest report, full of the Holy Ghost and wisdom, whom we may appoint over this business. But we will give ourselves continually to prayer, and to the ministry of the word.

And the saying pleased the whole multitude: and they chose Stephen, a man full of faith and of the Holy Ghost; and Philip, and Prochorus, and Nicanor, and Timon, and Parmenas, and Nicolas a proselyte of Antioch: Whom they set before the apostles: and when they had prayed, they laid their hands on them. And the word of God increased ; and the number of the disciples multiplied in Jerusalem greatly; and a great company of the priests were obedient to the faith.—*Acts* vi. 1–7.

Likewise must the deacons be grave, not double-tongued, not given to much wine, not greedy of filthy lucre ; holding the mystery of the faith in a pure conscience. And let these also first be proved ; then let them use the office of a deacon, being found blameless. Even so must their wives be grave, not slanderers, sober, faithful in all things. Let the deacons be the husband of one wife, ruling their children and their own houses well. For they that have used the office of a deacon well, purchase to themselves a good degree and great boldness in the faith which is in Christ Jesus.—1 *Tim.* iii. 8–13.

CHURCHES.*

I.

THEN they that feared the Lord spake often one to another; and the Lord hearkened, and heard it, and a book of remembrance was written before him for them that feared the Lord, and that thought upon his name. And they shall be mine, saith the Lord of hosts, in that day when I make up my jewels; and I will spare them, as a man spareth his own son that serveth him.—*Mal.* iii. 16, 17.

Now there are diversities of gifts, but the same Spirit. And there are differences of administrations, but the same Lord. And there are diversities of operations, but it is the same God which worketh all in all. But the manifestation of the Spirit is given to every man to profit withal. And God hath set some in the church, first apostles, secondarily prophets, thirdly teachers, after that miracles, then gifts of healings, helps, governments, diversities of tongues. Are

---

*This section is designed for use at the organization, or recognition of churches.

all apostles? are all prophets? are all teachers?
are all workers of miracles? have all the gifts of
healing? do all speak with tongues? do all in-
terpret? But covet earnestly the best gifts: and
yet shew I unto you a more excellent way.—1
Cor. xii. 4–7, 28–31.

Now therefore ye are no more strangers and
foreigners, but fellow-citizens with the saints,
and of the household of God; and are built upon
the foundation of the apostles and prophets,
Jesus Christ himself being the chief corner
stone; in whom all the building, fitly framed
together, groweth unto a holy temple in the
Lord: in whom ye also are builded together in
a habitation of God through the Spirit.—*Eph.*
i. 19–22.

Brethren, if a man be overtaken in a fault, ye
which are spiritual, restore such a one in the
spirit of meekness; considering thyself, lest
thou also be tempted. Bear ye one another's
burdens, and so fulfill the law of Christ.—
Gal. vi. 1, 2

A new commandment I give unto you, that ye
love one another; as I have loved you, that ye
also love one another. By this shall all men
know that ye are my disciples, if ye have love
one to another.—*John* xiii. 34, 35.

Let not then your good be evil spoken of: for
the kingdom of God is not meat and drink; but

righteousness, and peace and joy in the Holy
Spirit. For he that in these things serveth
Christ is acceptable to God, and approved of
men. Let us therefore follow after the things
which make for peace, and things wherewith
one may edify another.—*Rom.* xiv. 16–19.

If any man teach otherwise, and consent not
to wholesome words, even the words of our Lord
Jesus Christ, and to the doctrine which is according to godliness; he is proud, knowing nothing, but doting about questions and strifes of
words, whereof cometh envy, strife, railings,
evil surmisings, perverse disputings of men of
corrupt minds, and destitute of the truth, supposing that gain is godliness: from such withdraw thyself.—1 *Tim.* vi. 3–5.

If there be therefore any consolation in Christ,
if any comfort of love, if any fellowship of the
Spirit, if any bowels and mercies, fulfill ye my
joy, that ye be like-minded, having the same
love, being of one accord, of one mind. Let nothing be done through strife or vain-glory ; but
in lowliness of mind let each esteem other
better than themselves. Look not every man
on his own things, but every man also on the
things of others. Let this mind be in you, which
was also in Christ Jesus.—*Eph.* ii. 1–5.

Now to him that is of power to establish you
according to my gospel, and the preaching of

Jesus Christ according to the revelation of the mystery, which was kept secret since the world began, but now is made manifest, and by the scriptures of the prophets, according to the commandment of the everlasting God, made known to all nations for the obedience of faith ; to God only wise, be glory through Jesus Christ for ever. Amen.—*Rom.* xvi. 25–27.

The grace of the Lord Jesus Christ and the love of God, and the communion of the Holy Spirit be with you all. Amen.—**1** *Cor.* **xiii. 14.**

DEDICATIONS.

I.

HOW amiable are thy tabernacles, O Lord of hosts! My soul longeth, yea, even fainteth for the courts of the Lord: my heart and my flesh crieth out for the living God. Yea, the sparrow hath found a house, and the swallow a nest for herself, where she may lay her young, even thy altars, O Lord of hosts, my King, and my God. Blessed are they that dwell in thy house: they will still be praising thee. Blessed is the man whose strength is in thee; in whose heart are the ways of them. Who passing through the valley of Baca make it a well; the rain also filleth the pools. They go from strength to strength, every one of them in Zion appeareth before God.

O Lord God of hosts, hear my prayer: give ear, O God of Jacob. Behold, O God our shield, and look upon the face of thy anointed. For a day in thy courts is better than a thousand. I had rather be a doorkeeper in the house of my God, than to dwell in the tents of wickedness. For the Lord God is a sun and shield: the Lord

10

will give grace and glory ; no good thing will
he withhold from them that walk uprightly.   O
Lord of hosts, blessed is the man that trusteth
in thee.—*Psalm* lxxxiv. 1–12.

One thing have I desired of the Lord, that
will I seek after ; that I may dwell in the house
of the Lord all the days of my life, to behold the
beauty of the Lord, and to enquire in his temple.
For in the time of trouble he shall hide me in
his pavilion : in the secret of his tabernacle
shall he hide me : he shall set me up upon a
rock.—*Psalm* xxvii. 4, 5.

We have thought of thy lovingkindness, O
God, in the midst of thy temple.   According to
thy name, O God, so is thy praise unto the ends
of the earth : thy right hand is full of righteousness.   Let mount Zion rejoice, let the daughters of Judah be glad, because of thy judgments.
Walk about Zion, and go round about her : tell
the towers thereof.   Mark ye well her bulwarks,
consider her palaces; that ye may tell it to the
generation following.   For this God is our God
for ever and ever : he will be our guide even
unto death.—*Psalm* xlviii. 9–14.

Make a joyful noise unto the Lord, all ye
lands.   Serve the Lord with gladness : come before his presence with singing.   Know ye that
the Lord he is God : it is he that hath made us,
and not we ourselves ; we are his people, and

the sheep of his pasture. Enter into his gates
with thanksgiving, and into his courts with
praise : be thankful unto him, and bless his name.
For the Lord is good ; his mercy is everlasting,
and his truth endureth to all generations.—
Psalm c. 1–5.

I was glad when they said unto me, Let us go
into the house of the Lord. Our feet shall
stand within thy gates, O Jerusalem. Jerusalem is builded as a city that is compact together. Whither the tribes go up, the tribes of the
Lord, unto the testimony of Israel, to give
thanks unto the name of the Lord. For there
are set thrones of judgment, the thrones of the
house of David. Pray for the peace of Jerusalem : they shall prosper that love thee. Peace
be within thy walls, and prosperity within thy
palaces. For my brethren and companions'
sakes, I will now say, Peace be within thee.
Because of the house of the Lord our God I will
seek thy good.—*Psalm* cxxii. 1–9.

II.

Blessed be thou, Lord God of Israel our father,
for ever and ever. Thine, O Lord, is the greatness, and the power, and the glory, and the
victory, and the majesty: for all that is in the
heaven and in the earth is thine; thine is the
kingdom, O Lord, and thou art exalted as the

head above all.   Both riches and honor come
of thee, and thou reignest over all; and in thy
hand is power, and might; and in thy hand it
is to make great, and to give strength unto all.

Now therefore, our God, we thank thee, and
praise thy glorious name.   For we are strangers
before thee, and sojourners, as were all our
fathers: our days on the earth are as a shadow,
and there is none abiding.   O Lord our God, all
this store that we have prepared to build thee
a house for thy holy name cometh of thy
hand, and is all thy own.   I know also, my God,
that thou triest the heart, and hast pleasure
in uprightness.

As for me, in the uprightness of my heart I
have willingly offered all these things: and now
have I seen with joy thy people, which are present here, to offer willingly unto thee.   O Lord
God of Abraham, Isaac, and of Israel, our
fathers, keep this for ever in the imagination of
the thoughts of the heart of thy people, and
prepare their heart unto thee: and give a perfect heart, to keep thy commandments, thy testimonies, and thy statutes.—1 *Chron.* xxix. 10–13,
15–19.

The Lord hath said that he would dwell in
the thick darkness.   But I have built a house
of habitation for thee, and a place for thy dwelling for ever.   Blessed be the Lord God of Israel,

who hath with his hands fulfilled that which he spake with his mouth. O Lord God of Israel, there is no God like thee in the heaven, nor in the earth; which keepest covenant, and showest mercy unto thy servants, that walk before thee with all their hearts.

O Lord God of Israel, let thy word be verified which thou hast spoken unto thy servant. But will God in very deed dwell with men on the earth? Behold, heaven and the heaven of heavens cannot contain thee; how much less this house which I have built! Have respect therefore to the prayer of thy servant, and to his supplication, O Lord my God, to hearken unto the cry and the prayer which thy servant prayeth before thee.

That thy eyes may be open upon this house day and night, upon the place whereof thou hast said that thou wouldst put thy name there; to hearken unto the prayer which thy servant prayeth toward this place. Hear thou from the heavens, even from thy dwelling place, their prayer and their supplications, and maintain their cause, and forgive thy people which have sinned against thee.

Now, my God, let, I beseech thee, thy eyes be open, and let thy ears be attent unto the prayer that is made in this place. Arise, O Lord God, into thy resting place, thou, and the

10*

ark of thy strength: let thy priests, O Lord God, be clothed with salvation, and let thy saints rejoice in goodness.—2 *Chron.* vi. 1, 2, 4, 14, 17–20, 39–41.

BAPTISM.

I.

IN those days came John the Baptist, preaching in the wilderness of Judea, and saying, Repent ye : for the kingdom of heaven is at hand. For this is he that was spoken of by the prophet Isaiah, saying, The voice of one crying in the wilderness, Prepare ye the way of the Lord, make his paths straight. And the same John had his raiment of camel's hair, and a leathern girdle about his loins ; and his meat was locusts and wild honey. Then went out to him Jerusalem, and all Judea, and all the region round about Jordan, and were baptized of him in Jordan, confessing their sins.

But when he saw many of the Pharisees and Sadducees come to his baptism, he said unto them, O generation of vipers, who hath warned you to flee from the wrath to come ? Bring forth therefore fruits meet for repentance. And think not to say within yourselves, We have **Abraham** for our father : for I say unto you,

that God is able of these stones to raise up
children unto Abraham. And now also the
axe is laid unto the root of the trees: therefore
every tree which bringeth not forth good fruit
is hewn down, and cast into the fire. I indeed
baptize you with water unto repentance : but
he that cometh after me is mightier than I,
whose shoes I am not worthy to bear : he shall
baptize you with the Holy Ghost and with fire.
Whose fan is in his hand, and he will thoroughly
purge his floor, and gather his wheat into the
garner ; but he will burn up the chaff with
unquenchable fire.

Then cometh Jesus from Galilee to Jordan
unto John, to be baptized of him. But John
forbade him, saying, I have need to be baptized
of thee, and comest thou to me ? And Jesus
answering said unto him, Suffer it to be so now :
for thus it becometh us to fulfill all righteousness. Then he suffered him. And Jesus, when
he was baptized, went up straightway out of the
water: and lo, the heavens were opened unto
him, and he saw the Spirit of God descending
like a dove, and lighting upon him : and lo, a
voice from heaven, saying, This is my beloved
Son, in whom I am well pleased.—*Matt.* iii. 1–17.

II.

The beginning of the gospel of Jesus **Christ,**

the Son of God. As it is written in the prophets, Behold, I send my messenger before thy face, which shall prepare thy way before thee. The voice of one crying in the wilderness, Prepare ye the way of the Lord, make his paths straight. John did baptize in the wilderness, and preach the baptism of repentance for the remission of sins. And there went out unto him all the land of Judea, and they of Jerusalem, and were all baptized of him in the river of Jordan, confessing their sins.

And John was clothed with camel's hair, and with a girdle of skin about his loins; and he did eat locusts and wild honey; and preached, saying, There cometh one mightier than I after me, the latchet of whose shoes I am not worthy to stoop down and unloose. I indeed have baptized you with water: but he shall baptize you with the Holy Spirit.

And it came to pass in those days, that Jesus came from Nazareth of Galilee, and was baptized of John in Jordan. And straightway coming up out of the water, he saw the heavens opened, and the Spirit like a dove descending upon him: and there came a voice from heaven, saying, Thou art my beloved Son, in whom I am well pleased.—*Mark* i. 1–11.

And Jesus came and spake unto them, saying, All power is given unto me in heaven and in

earth. Go ye therefore, and teach all nations,
baptizing them in the name of the Father, and
of the Son, and of the Holy Ghost: teaching
them to observe all things, whatsoever I have
commanded you: and, lo, I am with you always,
even unto the end of the world. Amen.—*Matt.*
xxviii. 18–20.

Afterward he appeared unto the eleven as
they sat at meat, and upbraided them with their
unbelief and hardness of heart, because they believed not them which had seen him after he was
risen. And he said unto them, Go ye into all
the world, and preach the gospel to every creature. He that believeth and is baptized, shall be
saved; but he that believeth not, shall be damned. And these signs shall follow them that believe; in my name shall they cast out devils;
they shall speak with new tongues.—*Mark* xvi.
14–17.

Then Peter said unto them, Repent, and be
baptized every one of you in the name of Jesus
Christ, for the remission of sins, and ye shall
receive the gift of the Holy Ghost. For the
promise is unto you, and to your children, and to
all that are afar off, even as many as the Lord
our God shall call. And with many other words
did he testify and exhort, saying, Save yourselves
from this untoward generation.

Then they that gladly received his word, were

baptized: and the same day there were added unto them about three thousand souls. And they continued steadfastly in the apostles' doctrine and fellowship, and in breaking of bread and in prayers.—*Acts* ii. 38–42.

III.

And the angel of the Lord spake unto Philip, saying, Arise, and go toward the south, unto the way that goeth down from Jerusalem unto Gaza, which is desert. And he arose, and went: and behold, a man of Ethiopia, an eunuch of great authority under Candace queen of the Ethiopians, who had the charge of all her treasure, and had come to Jerusalem for to worship, was returning; and sitting in his chariot, read Esaias the prophet. Then the Spirit said unto Philip, Go near and join thyself to this chariot.

And Philip ran thither to him, and heard him read the prophet Esaias, and said, Understandest thou what thou readest? And he said, How can I, except some man should guide me? And he desired Philip that he would come up, and sit with him. The place of the scripture which he read was this, He was led as a sheep to the slaughter: and like a lamb dumb before his shearer, so opened he not his mouth: in his humiliation his judgment was taken away: and

who shall declare his generation? for his life is
taken from the earth. And the eunuch answered Philip, and said, I pray thee, of whom speak-
eth the prophet this? of himself, or of some
other man? Then Philip opened his mouth, and
began at the same scripture, and preached unto
him Jesus.

And as they went on their way they came
unto a certain water: and the eunuch said, See,
here is water; what doth hinder me to be baptized? And Philip said, If thou believest with
all thy heart, thou mayest. And he answered
and said, I believe that Jesus Christ is the son
of God. And he commanded the chariot to
stand still: and they went down both into the
water, both Philip and the eunuch; and he baptized him. And when they were come up out
of the water, the Spirit of the Lord caught
away Philip, that the eunuch saw him no more:
and he went on his way rejoicing.—*Acts* viii.
26–39.

While Peter yet spake these words, the Holy
Ghost fell on all them which heard the word.
And they of the circumcision which believed,
were astonished, as many as came with Peter,
because that on the Gentiles also was poured
out the gift of the Holy Ghost. For they heard
them speak with tongues, and magnify God
Then answered Peter, Can any man forbid water,

that these should not be baptized, which have received the Holy Ghost as well as we? And he commanded them to be baptized in the name of the Lord.—*Acts* x. 44–48.

IV.

And at midnight Paul and Silas prayed, and sang praises unto God : and the prisoners heard them. And suddenly there was a great earthquake, so that the foundations of the prison were shaken : and immediately all the doors were opened, and every one's bands were loosed. And the keeper of the prison awaking out of his sleep, and seeing the prison doors open, he drew out his sword, and would have killed himself, supposing that the prisoners had been fled. But Paul cried with a loud voice, saying, Do thyself no harm ; for we are all here.

Then he called for a light, and sprang in, and came trembling, and fell down before Paul and Silas, and brought them out, and said, Sirs, what must I do to be saved? And they said, Believe on the Lord Jesus Christ, and thou shalt be saved, and thy house. And they spake unto him the word of the Lord, and to all that were in his house. And he took them the same hour of the night, and washed their stripes ; and was baptized, he and all his, straightway. And when he had brought them into his house, he set **meat**

11

before them, and rejoiced, believing in God with all his house.—*Acts* xvi. 25–34.

And on the sabbath we went out of the city by a river side, where prayer was wont to be made ; and we sat down, and spake unto the women which resorted thither.

And a certain woman named Lydia, a seller of purple, of the city of Thyatira, which worshipped God, heard us ; whose heart the Lord opened, that she attended unto the things which were spoken of Paul. And when she was baptized, and her household, she besought us, saying, If ye have judged me to be faithful to the Lord, come into my house, and abide there.—*Acts* xvi. 13–15.

Know ye not, that so many of us as were baptized into Jesus Christ, were baptized into his death ? Therefore we are buried with him by baptism into death : that like as Christ was raised up from the dead by the glory of the Father, even so we also should walk in newness of life.—*Rom.* vi. 3, 4.

Buried with him in baptism, wherein also ye are risen with him through the faith of the operation of God, who hath raised him from the dead. —*Colossians* ii. 12.

For as many of you as have been baptized into Christ, have put on Christ.—*Gal.* iii. 27.

Repent, and be baptized every one of you in

the name of Jesus Christ, for the remission of sins, and ye shall receive the gift of the Holy Ghost. For the promise is unto you, and to your children, and to all that are afar off, even as many as the Lord our God shall call.—*Acts* ii. 38, 39.

THE LORD'S SUPPER.

I.

NOW the first day of the feast of unleavened
bread, the disciples came to Jesus, saying
unto him, Where wilt thou that we prepare for
thee to eat the passover? And he said, Go into
the city to such a man, and say unto him, The
Master saith, My time is at hand; I will keep
the passover at thy house with my disciples.
And the disciples did as Jesus had appointed
them, and they made ready the passover. Now
when the even was come, he sat down with the
twelve. And as they did eat he said, Verily
I say unto you, that one of you shall betray me.
And they were exceeding sorrowful, and began every one of them to say unto him, Lord is
it I? And he answered and said, He that
dippeth his hand with me in the dish, the same
shall betray me. The Son of man goeth as it
is written of him : but wo unto that man by
whom the Son of man is betrayed ! It had been
good for that man if he had not been born.
Then Judas, which betrayed him, answered and

said, Master, is it I ?   He said unto him, Thou
hast said.

And as they were eating, Jesus took bread and
blessed *it*, and brake it, and gave it to the disciples, and said, Take, eat; this is my body.
And he took the cup, and gave thanks, and gave
it to them, saying, Drink ye all of it; for this
is my blood of the new testament, which is shed
for many for the remission of sins.   But I say
unto you, I will not drink henceforth of this
fruit of the vine, until that day when I drink it
new with you in my Father's kingdom.   And
when they had sung a hymn, they went out into
the mount of Olives.—*Matt.* xxvi. 17–30.

II.

And the first day of unleavened bread, when
they killed the passover, his disciples said unto
him, Where wilt thou that we go and prepare
that thou mayest eat the passover?   And he
sendeth forth two of his disciples, and saith
unto them, Go ye into the city, and there shall
meet you a man bearing a pitcher of water: follow him.   And wheresoever he shall go in, say
ye to the good man of the house, The Master
saith, Where is the guest-chamber, where I
shall eat the passover with my disciples?   And
he will show you a large upper room furnished
and prepared: there make ready for us.   And

his disciples went forth and came into the city,
and found as he had said unto them: and they
made ready the passover. And in the evening
he cometh with the twelve. And as they sat
and did eat, Jesus said, Verily I say unto you,
one of you which eateth with me shall betray
me. And they began to be sorrowful, and to
say unto him one by one, Is it I? and another
said, Is it I? And he answered and said unto
them, It is one of the twelve, that dippeth with
me in the dish. The Son of man indeed goeth,
as it is written of him; but wo to that man by
whom the Son of man is betrayed! good were
it for that man if he had never been born.

And as they did eat, Jesus took bread, and
blessed, and brake it, and gave to them, and
said, Take, eat; this is my body. And he took
the cup, and when he had given thanks he gave it
to them: and they all drank of it. And he said
unto them, This is my blood of the new testament, which is shed for many. Verily I say unto
you, I will drink no more of the fruit of the vine,
until that day that I drink it new in the kingdom
of God. And when they had sung a hymn, they
went out into the mount of Olives.—*Mark* xiv.
12–26.

III.

Then came the day of unleavened bread, when

the passover must be killed. And he sent
Peter and John, saying, Go and prepare us the
passover, that we may eat. And they said unto him, Where wilt thou that we prepare ? And
he said unto them, Behold, when ye are entered into the city, there shall a man meet you,
bearing a pitcher of water; follow him into the
house where he entereth in. And ye shall say
unto the good man of the house, The Master
saith unto thee, Where is the guest-chamber,
where I shall eat the passover with my disciples ? And he shall shew you a large upper
room furnished; there make ready. And they
went, and found as he had said unto them:
and they made ready the passover. And when
the hour was come, he sat down, and the twelve
apostles with him. And he said unto them, With
desire I have desired to eat this passover with you
before I suffer : for I say unto you, I will not any
more eat thereof, until it be fulfilled in the kingdom of God. And he took the cup, and gave
thanks, and said, Take this, and divide it among
yourselves : for I say unto you, I will not drink
of the fruit of the vine, until the kingdom of
God shall come.

And he took bread, and gave thanks, and
brake it, and gave unto them, saying, This is
my body which is given for you : this do in remembrance of me. Likewise also the cup after

supper, saying, This cup is the new testament
in my blood, which is shed for you. But behold, the hand of him that betrayeth me is with
me on the table. And truly the Son of man
goeth, as it was determined: but wo unto that
man by whom he is betrayed!—*Luke* xxii. 7–22.

IV.

For I have received of the Lord that which
also I delivered unto you, That the Lord Jesus,
the same night in which he was betrayed, took
bread: and when he had given thanks, he brake
it, and said, Take, eat: this is my body, which
is broken for you: this do in remembrance of
me. After the same manner, also, he took the
cup, when he had supped, saying, This cup is
the new testament in my blood: this do ye, as
oft as ye drink it, in remembrance of me. For
as often as ye eat this bread, and drink this cup,
ye do show the Lord's death till he come.

Wherefore, whosoever shall eat this bread,
and drink this cup of the Lord, unworthily, shall
be guilty of the body and blood of the Lord.
But let a man examine himself, and so let him
eat of that bread, and drink of that cup. For
he that eateth and drinketh unworthily, eateth
and drinketh damnation to himself, not discern-
ing the Lord's body. For this cause many are
weak and sickly among you, and many sleep.—
1 *Cor.* xi. 23–30.

MARRIAGE.*

I.

AND the Lord God said, It is not good that the man should be alone : I will make him an help meet for him. And the Lord God caused a deep sleep to fall upon Adam, and he slept; and he took one of his ribs, and closed up the flesh instead thereof: and of the rib, which the Lord God had taken from man, made he a woman, and brought her unto the man.

And Adam said, This is now bone of my bones, and flesh of my flesh : she shall be called Woman, because she was taken out of man. Therefore shall a man leave his father and his mother, and shall cleave unto his wife : and they shall be one flesh.—*Gen.* ii. 18, 21–24.

Whoso findeth a wife, findeth a good thing, and obtaineth favor of the Lord.—*Prov* xviii. 22.

A virtuous woman is a crown to her husband : but she that maketh ashamed is as rottenness in his bones.—*Prov.* xii. 4.

* For Forms of Marriage Service see p. 205.

Who can find a virtuous woman? for her price is far above rubies. The heart of her husband doth safely trust in her, so that he shall have no need of spoil. She will do him good and not evil all the days of her life. She is like the merchants' ships; she bringeth her food from afar. She stretcheth out her hand to the poor; yea, she reacheth forth her hands to the needy. Her husband is known in the gates, when he sitteth among the elders of the land.

Strength and honor are her clothing; and she shall rejoice in time to come. She openeth her mouth with wisdom; and in her tongue is the law of kindness. She looketh well to the ways of her household, and eateth not the bread of idleness. Her children arise up, and call her blessed; her husband also, and he praiseth her. Many daughters have done virtuously, but thou excellest them all. Favor is deceitful, and beauty is vain: but a woman that feareth the Lord, she shall be praised.—*Prov.* xxxi. 10–12, 14, 20, 23, 25–30.

II.

Wives, submit yourselves unto your own husbands, as it is fit in the Lord. Husbands, love your wives, and be not bitter against them.—*Col.* iii. 18, 19.

Wives, submit yourselves unto your own hus-

bands, as unto the Lord. For the husband is
the head of the wife, even as Christ is the head
of the church : and he is the saviour of the body.
Therefore as the church is subject unto Christ,
so let the wives be to their own husbands in every thing. Husbands, love your wives, even as
Christ also loved the church, and gave himself
for it ; that he might sanctify and cleanse it
with the washing of water by the word, that he
might present it to himself a glorious church,
not having spot, or wrinkle, or any such thing ;
but that it should be holy and without blemish.

So ought men to love their wives as their own
bodies. He that loveth his wife loveth himself.
For no man ever yet hated his own flesh ; but
nourisheth and cherisheth it, even as the Lord
the church : for we are members of his body,
of his flesh, and of his bones. For this cause
shall a man leave his father and mother, and
shall be joined unto his wife, and they two shall
be one flesh. This is a great mystery : but I
speak concerning Christ and the church. Nevertheless, let every one of you in particular so
love his wife even as himself ; and the wife see
that she reverence her husband.—*Eph.* v. 22–33

For the man is not of the woman, but the
woman of the man. Neither was the man cre-
ated for the woman, but the woman for the man.
Nevertheless, neither is the man without the

woman, neither the woman without the man, in the Lord. For as the woman is of the man, even so is the man also by the woman; but all things of God.—1 *Cor.* xi. 8, 9, 11, 12.

III.

Likewise, ye wives, be in subjection to your own husbands; that, if any obey not the word, they also may without the word be won by the conversation of the wives; while they behold your chaste conversation coupled with fear. Whose adorning, let it not be that outward adorning, of plaiting the hair, and of wearing of gold, or of putting on apparel; but let it be the hidden man of the heart, in that which is not corruptible, even the ornament of a meek and quiet spirit, which is in the sight of God of great price.

For after this manner in the old time the holy women also, who trusted in God, adorned themselves, being in subjection unto their own husbands: even as Sarah obeyed Abraham, calling him lord: whose daughters ye are, as long as ye do well, and are not afraid with any amazement. Likewise, ye husbands, dwell with them according to knowledge, giving honor unto the wife, as unto the weaker vessel, and as being heirs together of the grace of life; that your prayers be not hindered.—1 *Pet.* iii. 1–7.

Let the husband render unto the wife due benevolence : and likewise also the wife unto the husband.—1 *Cor.* vii. 3.

And he answered and said unto them, Have ye not read, that he which made them at the beginning, made them male and female, and said, for this cause shall a man leave father and mother, and shall cleave to his wife ; and they twain shall be one flesh ? Wherefore, they are no more twain, but one flesh. What therefore God hath joined together, let no man put asunder.— *Matt.* xix. 4–6.

For the woman which hath a husband, is bound by the law to her husband so long as he liveth ; but if the husband be dead, she is loosed from the law of her husband. So then if, while her husband liveth, she be married to another man, she shall be called an adulteress : but if her husband be dead, she is free from that law ; so that she is no adulteress, though she be married to another man.—*Rom.* vii. 2, 3.

Live joyfully with the wife whom thou lovest all the days of the life of thy vanity, which he hath given thee under the sun, all the days of thy vanity : for that is thy portion in this life, and in thy labor which thou takest under the sun.—*Eccl.* ix. 9.

In the resurrection they neither marry, nor

12

are given in marriage, but are as the angels of God in heaven.—*Matt.* ii. 30.

The time is short. It remaineth, that both they that have wives, be as though they had none; and they that weep, as though they wept not; and they that rejoice, as though they rejoiced not; and they that buy, as though they possessed not; and they that use this world, as not abusing it. For the fashion of this world passeth away.—1 *Cor.* vii. 29–31.

TEMPERANCE.

WINE is a mocker, strong drink is raging: and whosoever is deceived thereby is not wise.—*Prov.* xx. 1.

Come ye, say they, I will fetch wine, and we will fill ourselves with strong drink; and to-morrow shall be as this day, and much more abundant.—*Isa.* xxxvi. 12.

Be not among winebibbers; among riotous eaters of flesh : For the drunkard and the glutton shall come to poverty : and drowsiness shall clothe a man with rags.—*Prov.* xxiii. 20, 21.

Wo unto him that giveth his neighbor drink, that puttest thy bottle to him, and makest him drunken also, that thou mayest look on their nakedness ! Thou art filled with shame for glory : drink thou also, and let thy foreskin be uncovered : the cup of the Lord's right hand shall be turned unto thee, and shameful spewing shall be on thy glory.—*Hab.* ii. 15, 16.

Wo unto them that rise up early in the morning, that they may follow strong drink; that continue until night, till wine inflame them ! And the harp, and the viol, the tabret, and pipe,

and wine, are in their feasts: but they regard
not the work of the Lord, neither consider the
operation of his hands. Wo unto them that
are mighty to drink wine, and men of strength
to mingle strong drink: which justify the wicked
for reward, and take away the righteousness of
the righteous from him!—*Isa.* v. 11, 12, 22, 23.

Who hath wo? who hath sorrow? who hath
contentions? who hath babbling? who hath
wounds without cause? who hath redness of
eyes? They that tarry long at the wine; they
that go to seek mixed wine. Look not thou
upon the wine when it is red, when it giveth his
color in the cup, when it moveth itself aright.
At the last it biteth like a serpent, and stingeth
like an adder.—*Prov.* xxiii. 29–32.

Woe to the crown of pride, to the drunk-
ards of Ephraim, whose glorious beauty is a
fading flower, which are overcome with wine
They also have erred through wine, and
through strong drink are out of the way. The
priests and the prophet have erred through
strong drink, they are swallowed up of wine,
they are out of the way through strong drink;
they err in vision, they stumble in judgment.
—*Isa.* xxxiii. 1, 3. 11.

Do not drink wine nor strong drink, thou
nor thy sons with thee, when ye go into the
tabernacle of the congregation, lest ye die. It
shall be a statute forever throughout your
generations.—*Lev.* x. 9.

HUMAN FRAILTY.*

MAN that is born of a woman is of few days, and full of trouble. He cometh forth like a flower, and is cut down: he fleeth also as a shadow, and continueth not. And dost thou open thy eyes upon such a one, and bringest me into judgment with thee? Who can bring a clean thing out of an unclean? not one. Seeing his days are determined, the number of his months are with thee, thou hast appointed his bounds that he cannot pass; turn from him, that he may rest, till he shall accomplish, as a hireling, his day.

For there is hope of a tree, if it be cut down, that it will sprout again, and that the tender branch thereof will not cease. Though the root thereof wax old in the earth, and the stock thereof die in the ground; yet through the scent of water it will bud, and bring forth boughs like a plant. But man dieth, and wasteth away: yea, man giveth up the ghost, and where is he? As

---

* The following several sections are fitted for funeral services, and for the visitation of the sick.

12*

the waters fail from the sea, and the flood de-
cayeth and drieth up, so man lieth down and
riseth not: till the heavens be no more, they
shall not awake, nor be raised out of their
sleep.—*Job* xiv. 1–12.

Now my days are swifter than a post: they
flee away, they see no good. They are passed
away as the swift ships: as the eagle that has-
teth to the prey. If I say, I will forget my complaint, I will leave off my heaviness, and comfort myself: I am afraid of all my sorrows, I
know that thou wilt not hold me innocent.—
Job ix. 25–28.

As for man, his days are as grass: as a flower
of the field, so he flourisheth. For the wind
passeth over it, and it is gone; and the place
thereof shall know it no more.—*Psalm* ciii.
15, 16.

Shall mortal man be more just than God?
shall a man be more pure than his Maker? Behold, he put no trust in his servants; and his
angels he charged with folly: how much less in
them that dwell in houses of clay, whose foundation is in the dust, which are crushed before
the moth? They are destroyed from morning
to evening: they perish for ever without any
regarding it? Doth not their excellency which
is in them go away? they die, even without
wisdom.—*Job* iv. 17–21.

Go to now, ye that say, to-day or to-morrow we will go into such a city, and continue there a year, and buy, and sell, and get gain : whereas ye know not what shall be on the morrow. For what is your life? It is even a vapor, that appeareth for a little time, and then vanisheth away. For that ye ought to say, If the Lord will, we shall live, and do this, or that.—*James* iv. 13–15.

But this I say, brethren, the time is short : it remaineth, that both they that have wives be as though they had none ; and they that wept as though they wept not ; and they that rejoice as though they rejoiced not ; and they that buy as though they possessed not ; and they that use this world as not abusing it ; for the fashion of this world passeth away.—1 *Cor.* vii. 29–31.

See then that ye walk circumspectly, not as fools, but as wise, redeeming the time, because the days are evil.—*Eph.* v. 15, 16.

Lord, make me to know my end, and the measure of my days, what it is; that I may know how frail I am. Behold, thou hast made my days as a hand-breadth ; and my age is as nothing before thee ; verily every man at his best state is altogether vanity.—*Psalm* xxxix. 4, 5.

SICKNESS.

I SAID in the cutting off of my days, I shall
go to the gates of the grave: I am deprived
of the residue of my years.   I said, I shall not
see the Lord, even the Lord in the land of the
living: I shall behold man no more with the
inhabitants of the world.   My age is departed,
and is removed from me as a shepherd's tent: I
have cut off like a weaver my life: he will cut
me off with pining sickness: from day even till
night wilt thou make an end of me.

I reckoned till morning, that, as a lion, so will
he break all my bones: from day even to night
wilt thou make an end of me.   Like a crane or
a swallow, so did I chatter: I did mourn as a
dove: my eyes fail with looking upward: O
Lord, I am oppressed; undertake for me.
What shall I say?   He hath both spoken unto
me, and himself hath done it: I shall go softly
all my years in the bitterness of my soul.

O Lord, by these things men live, and in all
these things is the life of my spirit: so wilt
thou recover me and make me to live.   Behold,
for peace I had great bitterness: but thou hast

in love to my soul delivered it from the pit of corruption; for thou hast cast all my sins behind thy back. For the grave cannot praise thee, death cannot celebrate thee: they that go down into the pit cannot hope for thy truth.

I cried by reason of my affliction unto the Lord, and he heard me; out of the belly of hell cried I, and thou heardest my voice. For thou hadst cast me into the deep, in the midst of the seas; and the floods compassed me about: all thy billows and thy waves passed over me. Then I said, I am cast out of thy sight; yet I will look again toward thy holy temple. The waters compassed me about, even to the soul: the depth closed me round about, the weeds were wrapped about my head.

I went down to the bottoms of the mountains; the earth with her bars was about me for ever: yet hast thou brought up my life from corruption, O Lord my God. When my soul fainted within me I remembered the Lord: and my prayer came in unto thee, into thy holy temple. They that observe lying vanities forsake their own mercy: but I will sacrifice unto thee with the voice of thanksgiving; I will pay that that I have vowed. Salvation is of the Lord.— *Jonah* ii. 2–9.

DEATH.

I.

IS THERE not an appointed time to man upon earth ? are not his days also like the days of a hireling ? As a servant earnestly desireth the shadow, and as a hireling looketh for the reward of his work: so am I made to possess months of vanity, and wearisome nights are appointed to me. When I lie down, I say, When shall I arise, and the night be gone ? and I am full of tossings to and fro unto the dawning of the day.

My flesh is clothed with worms, and clods of dust ; my skin is broken, and become loathsome. My days are swifter than a weaver's shuttle, and are spent without hope. Oh remember that my life is wind : my eye shall no more see good. The eye of him that hath seen me shall see me no more : thy eyes are upon me, and I am not.

As the cloud is consumed and vanisheth away ; so he that goeth down to the grave shall come up no more. He shall return no more to

his house, neither shall his place know him
any more. Therefore I will not refrain my
mouth; I will speak in the anguish of my
spirit; I will complain in the bitterness of my
soul.—*Job* vii. 1–11.

One dieth in his full strength, being wholly
at ease and quiet. His breasts are full of milk,
and his bones are moistened with marrow. And
another dieth in the bitterness of his soul, and
never eateth with pleasure. They shall lie
down alike in the dust, and the worms shall
cover them.—*Job* xxi. 23–26.

Lord, thou hast been our dwelling place in
all generations. Before the mountains were
brought forth, or ever thou hadst formed the
earth, and the world, even from everlasting to
everlasting, thou art God. Thou turnest man
to destruction; and sayest, Return, ye children
of men.

For a thousand years in thy sight are but as
yesterday when it is passed, and as a watch in
the night. Thou carriest them away as with
a flood; they are as a sleep: in the morning
they are like grass which groweth up. In the
morning it flourisheth, and groweth up, in the
evening it is cut down and withered. For we
are consumed by thy anger, and by thy wrath
are we troubled. Thou hast set our iniquities
before thee, our secret sins in the light of thy
countenance.

For all our days are passed away in thy wrath: we spend our years as a tale that is told. The days of our years are threescore years and ten; and if by reason of strength they be fourscore years, yet is their strength labor and sorrow; for it is soon cut off and we fly away.—*Psalm* xc. 1–10.

II.

O Lord God of my salvation, I have cried day and night before thee: let my prayer come before thee: incline thy ear unto my cry; for my soul is full of troubles: and my life draweth nigh unto the grave. I am counted with them that go down into the pit: I am as a man that hath no strength: free among the dead, like the slain that lie in the grave, whom thou rememberest no more: and they are cut off from thy hand.

Thou hast laid me in the lowest pit, in darkness, in the deeps. Thy wrath lieth hard upon me, and thou hast afflicted me with all thy waves. Thou hast put away my acquaintance far from me; thou hast made me an abomination unto them: I am shut up, and I cannot come forth.

My eye mourneth by reason of affliction: Lord, I have called daily upon thee, I have

stretched out my hands unto thee. Wilt thou
show wonders to the dead? shall the dead arise
and praise thee? Shall thy lovingkindness be
declared in the grave? or thy faithfulness in
destruction? Shall thy wonders be known in
the dark? and the righteousness in the land of
forgetfulness?

But unto thee have I cried, O Lord; and in
the morning shall my prayer prevent thee.
Lord, why castest thou off my soul? why hidest
thou thy face from me? I am afflicted and
ready to die from my youth up: while I suffer
thy terrors I am distracted. Thy fierce wrath
goeth over me: thy terrors have cut me off.
They came round about me daily like water;
they compassed me about together. Lover
and friend hast thou put far from me, and my
acquaintance into darkness.—*Psalm* **lxxx. iii.**
1–18.

13

DEATH OF THE RIGHTEOUS.

I KNOW that my Redeemer liveth, and that he shall stand at the latter day upon the earth: and though after my skin worms destroy this body, yet in my flesh shall I see God: whom I shall see for myself, and my eyes shall behold, and not another; though my reins be consumed within me.—*Job* xix. 25–27.

Thou shalt guide me with thy counsel and afterward receive me to glory. Whom have I in heaven but thee? and there is none upon earth that I desire besides thee. My flesh and my heart faileth: but God is the strength of my heart, and my portion for ever.—*Psalm* lxxv. 24–26.

These things said he: and after that he saith unto them, Our friend Lazarus sleepeth; but I go, that I may awake him out of sleep. Then said his disciples, Lord, if he sleep, he shall do well. Howbeit, Jesus spake of his death: but they thought that he had spoken of taking of rest in sleep.—*John* xi. 11–13.

Let not your heart be troubled: ye believe in God, believe also in me. In my Father's house are many mansions: if it were not so I would have told you. I go to prepare a place for you.

And if I go and prepare a place for you, I will come again, and receive you unto myself; that where I am there ye may be also.—*John* xiv. 1–3.

Nay, in all these things we are more than conquerors through him that loved us. For I am persuaded, that neither death, nor life, nor angels, nor principalities, nor powers, nor things present, nor things to come, nor height, nor depth, nor any other creature, shall be able to separate us from the love of God, which is in Christ Jesus our Lord.—*Rom.* viii. 37–39.

For I am now ready to be offered, and the time of my departure is at hand. I have fought a good fight, I have finished my course, I have kept the faith; henceforth there is laid up for me a crown of righteousness, which the Lord, the righteous judge, shall give me at that day: and not to me only, but unto all them also that love his appearing.—2 *Tim.* iv. 6–8.

So when this corruptible shall have put on incorruption, and this mortal shall have put on immortality, then shall be brought to pass the saying that is written, Death is swallowed up in victory. O death, where is thy sting? O grave, where is thy victory? The sting of death is sin; and the strength of sin is the law. But thanks be to God, which giveth us the victory through our Lord Jesus Christ.—2 *Cor.* xiv. 54–57.

THE RESURRECTION.

A S touching the dead, that they rise: have ye not read in the book of Moses, how in the bush God spake unto him, saying, I am the God of Abraham, and the God of Isaac, and the God of Jacob? He is not the God of the dead, but the God of the living.—*Mark* xii. 26, 27.

Yea doubtless, and I count all things but loss for the excellency of the knowledge of Christ Jesus my Lord: for whom I have suffered the loss of all things, and do count them but dung, that I may win Christ, and be found in him, not having my own righteousness, which is of the law, but that which is through the faith of Christ, the righteousness which is of God by faith: that I may know him, and the power of his resurrection, and the fellowship of his sufferings, being made conformable unto his death; if by any means I might attain unto the resurrection of the dead.

For our conversation is in heaven; **from**

whence also we look for the Saviour, the Lord
Jesus Christ: who shall change our vile body,
that it may be fashioned like unto his glorious
body, according to the working whereby he is
able even to subdue all things unto himself.—
Phil. iii. 8–11, 20, 21.

I would not have you to be ignorant, brethren, concerning them which are asleep, that ye
sorrow not even as others which have no hope.
For if we believe that Jesus died and rose again,
even so them also which sleep in Jesus, will God
bring with him. For this we say unto you by
the word of the Lord, that we which are alive
and remain unto the coming of the Lord shall
not prevent them which are asleep.

For the Lord himself shall descend from heaven with a shout, with the voice of the archangel, and with the trump of God: and the dead
in Christ shall rise first: then we which are alive
and remain, shall be caught up together with
them in the clouds, to meet the Lord in the air:
and so shall we ever be with the Lord. Wherefore, comfort one another with these words.—
1 *Thess.* iv. 13–18.

II.

I will ransom them from the power of the
grave; I will redeem them from death: O death,
I will be thy plagues; O grave, I will be thy

13*

destruction : repentance shall be hid from my eyes.—*Hosea* xiii. 14.

Verily, verily, I say unto you, The hour is coming, and now is, when the dead shall hear the voice of the Son of God; and they that hear shall live. For as the Father hath life in himself; so hath he given to the Son to have life in himself; and hath given him authority to execute judgment also, because he is the Son of man. Marvel not at this : for the hour is coming, in the which all that are in the grave shall hear his voice and shall come forth ; they that have done good, unto the resurrection of life ; and they that have done evil, unto the resurrection of damnation.—*John* v. 25–29.

III.

Now if Christ be preached that he rose from the dead, how say some among you that there is no resurrection of the dead? But if there be no resurrection of the dead, then is Christ not risen : and if Christ be not risen, then is our preaching vain, and your faith is also vain. Yea, and we are found false witnesses of God ; because we have testified of God that he raised up Christ : whom he raised not up, if so be that the dead rise not.

For if the dead rise not, then is not Christ raised : and if Christ be not raised, your faith is vain; ye are yet in your sins. Then they also which are fallen asleep in Christ are perished. If in this life only we have hope in Christ, we are of all men most miserable. But now is Christ risen from the dead, and become the first fruits of them that slept. Christ the first fruits; afterwards they that are Christ's at his coming.

It is sown in corruption, it is raised in incorruption : it is sown in dishonor, it is raised in glory : it is sown in weakness, it is raised in power : it is sown a natural body, it is raised a spiritual body. There is a natural body, and there is a spiritual body. And so it is written, The first man Adam was made a living soul; the last Adam was made a quickening spirit.

Howbeit, that was not first which is spiritual, but that which is natural; and afterward that which is spiritual. The first man is of the earth, earthy : the second man is the Lord from heaven. As is the earthy, such are they also that are earthy: and as is the heavenly, such are they also that are heavenly. And as we have borne the image of the earthy, we shall also bear the image of the heavenly.

Now this I say, brethren, that flesh and blood cannot inherit the kingdom of God; neither doth corruption inherit incorruption. Behold, I shew you a mystery; We shall not all sleep, but we shall all be changed in a moment, in the twink-

ling of an eye, at the last trump : for the trumpet
shall sound, and the dead shall be raised incorruptible, and we shall be changed.   For this
corruptible must put on incorruption, and this
mortal must put on immortality.

So when this corruptible shall have put on
incorruption, and this mortal shall have put on
immortality, then shall be brought to pass the
saying that is written, Death is swallowed up in
victory.   O death, where is thy sting?   O grave,
where is thy victory?   The sting of death is
sin ; and the strength of sin is the law.

But thanks be to God, which giveth us the victory through our Lord Jesus Christ.   Therefore,
my beloved brethren, be ye steadfast, unmova-
ble, always abounding in the work of the Lord,
forasmuch as ye know that your labor is not in
vain in the Lord.—1 *Cor.* xv. 12–58.

THE RIGHTEOUS DEAD.

I.

AND I heard a voice from heaven saying unto me, Write, Blessed are the dead which die in the Lord from henceforth: Yea, saith the Spirit, that they may rest from their labors; and their works do follow them.—*Rev.* xiv. 13.

In my Father's house are many mansions: if it were not so, I would have told you. I go to prepare a place for you. And if I go and prepare a place for you, I will come again, and receive you unto myself; that where I am, there ye may be also.—*John* xiv. 2, 3.

As it is written, Eye hath not seen, nor ear heard, neither have entered into the heart of man, the things which God hath prepared for them that love him. But God hath revealed them unto us by his Spirit: for the Spirit searcheth all things, yea, the deep things of God.—1 *Cor.* ii. 9, 10.

Then shall the King say unto them on his right hand, Come, ye blessed of my Father, inherit the kingdom prepared for you from the foundation of the world: for I was a hungered,

and ye gave me meat: I was thirsty, and ye
gave me drink: I was a stranger, and ye took
me in: naked and ye clothed me: I was sick,
and ye visited me: I was in prison, and ye came
unto me.

Then shall the righteous answer him, saying,
Lord, when saw we thee a hungered, and fed
thee? or thirsty, and gave thee drink? when
saw we thee a stranger, and took thee in? or
naked, and clothed thee? or when saw we thee
sick, or in prison, and came unto thee? and the
King shall answer and say unto them, Verily I
say unto you, Inasmuch as ye have done it unto
one of the least of these my brethren, ye have
done it unto me.—*Matt.* xxv. 34-40.

And Jesus said unto them, Verily I say unto
you, That ye which have followed me, in the regeneration, when the Son of man shall sit in the
throne of his glory, ye also shall sit upon twelve
thrones, judging the twelve tribes of Israel.
And every one that hath forsaken houses, or
brethren, or sisters, or father, or mother, or wife,
or children, or lands, for my name's sake, shall
receive a hundredfold, and shall inherit everlasting life.—*Matt.* xix. 28, 29.

These are they which came out of great tribulation, and have washed their robes, and made
them white in the blood of the Lamb.   Therefore are they before the throne of God, and

serve him day and night in his temple: and he
that sitteth on the throne shall dwell among
them. They shall hunger no more, neither
thirst any more; neither shall the sun light on
them, nor any heat. For the Lamb which is in
the midst of the throne shall feed them, and
shall lead them unto living fountains of waters:
and God shall wipe away all tears from their
eyes.—*Rev.* vii. 14–17.

II.

And I saw a new heaven and a new earth:
for the first heaven and the first earth were
passed away; and there was no more sea. And
I John saw the holy city, new Jerusalem, coming down from God out of heaven, prepared as
a bride adorned for her husband.

And I heard a great voice out of heaven
saying, Behold, the tabernacle of God is with
men, and he will dwell with them, and they
shall be his people, and God himself shall
be with them, and be their God. And God
shall wipe away all tears from their eyes; and
there shall be no more death, neither sorrow,
nor crying, neither shall there be any more
pain: for the former things are passed away.

And he that sat upon the throne said, Behold,
I make all things new. And he said unto me,
Write: for these words are true and faithful.

HOPE OF THE RIGHTEOUS.

FOR we know that if our earthly house of this tabernacle were dissolved, we have a building of God, a house not made with hands, eternal in the heavens. For in this we groan, earnestly desiring to be clothed upon with our house which is from heaven: if so be that being clothed we shall not be found naked. For we that are in this tabernacle do groan, being burdened: not for that we would be unclothed, but clothed upon, that mortality might be swallowed up of life. Now he that hath wrought us for the self-same thing is God, who also hath given unto us the earnest of the Spirit. Therefore we are always confident, knowing that, whilst we are at home in the body, we are absent from the Lord. We are confident, I say, and willing rather to be absent from the body, and to be present with the Lord. Wherefore we labor, that, whether present or absent, we may be accepted of him.—2 *Cor.* v. 1–9.

For which cause we faint not; but though our outward man perish, yet the inward man is renewed day by day. For our light affliction, which is but for a moment, worketh for us a far more exceeding and eternal weight of glory; while we look not at the things which are seen, but at the things which are not seen: for the things which are seen are temporal; but the things which are not seen are eternal. —2 *Cor.* iv. 16–18.

If ye then be risen with Christ seek those which are above, where Christ sitteth at the right hand of God. Set your affections on things above, not on things on the earth. For ye are dead, and your life is hid with Christ in God. When Christ, who is our life, shall appear, then shall ye also appear with him in glory.—*Col.* iii. 1–4.

For, if we believe that Jesus died and rose again, even so them also which sleep in Jesus will God bring with him. For the Lord himself shall descend from heaven with a shout, with the voice of the archangel, and with the trump of God: and the dead in Christ shall rise first. Then we which are alive and remain shall be caught up together with them in the clouds, to meet the Lord in the air; and so shall we ever be with the Lord. Wherefore comfort one another with these words.—1 *Thess.* iv. 14–18.

DEATH OF A CHILD.

OH my God, my soul is cast down within
me.   All thy waves and thy billows are
gone over me.—*Ps.* xlii. 6, 7.

Behold and see if there be any sorrow like
unto my sorrow, which is done unto me, wherewith the Lord hath afflicted me?—*Lam.* i. 12.

The Lord will not cast off forever.   But
though he cause grief, yet will he have compassion, according to the multitude of his
mercies.   For he doth not afflict willingly, nor
grieve the children of men.—*Lam.* iii. 31-33.

Like as a father pitieth his children, so the
Lord pitieth them that fear him.   For he
knoweth our frame; he remembereth that we
are dust.—*Ps.* ciii. 13, 14.

And they brought young children to him
that he should touch them : and his disciples
rebuked them that brought them.   But when
Jesus saw it, he was much displeased, and
said unto them, Suffer the little children to
come unto me, and forbid them not; for of
such is the kingdom of God.   Verily, I say
unto you, whosoever shall not receive the
kingdom of God as a little child, he shall not
enter therein.   And he took them up in his
arms, put his hands upon them, and blessed
them. —*Mark* x. 13-16

And he took a child and set him in the
midst of them; and when he had taken him
in his arms, he said unto them, Whosoever
shall receive one of such children in my name
receiveth me; and whosoever receiveth me,
receiveth not me, but him that sent me.—
Mark ix. 36, 37.

And Jesus called a little child unto him,
and set him in the midst of them, and said,
Verily I say unto you, except ye be converted and become as little children, ye shall not
enter into the kingdom of heaven. Whosoever therefore shall humble himself as this
little child, the same is greatest in the kingdom of heaven.—*Matt.* xviii. 2–4.

And Hagar went and sat her down over
against him, a good way off, for she said, Let
me not see the death of the child. And she
sat over against him, and lifted up her voice
and wept.—*Gen.* xxi. 16.

For this child I prayed; and the Lord hath
given me my petition which I asked of him;
therefore also I have lent him to the Lord.—
1 *Sam.* i. 27, 28.

And the Lord struck the child, and it was
very sick. David therefore besought God for
the child, and fasted, and went in and lay all
night upon the earth. And it came to pass

on the seventh day, that the child died
Therefore David said unto his servants, Is the
child dead? And they said, He is dead.
Then David arose from the earth, and changed
his apparel, and came into the house of the
Lord, and worshipped. And he said, While
the child was yet alive, I fasted and wept;
for I said, Who can tell whether God will be
gracious to me, that the child may live? But
now he is dead, wherefore should I fast?
Can I bring him back again? I shall go to
him, but he shall not return to me.—2 *Sam.*
xii. 15–23.

While Jesus yet spake, there came from
the ruler of the synagogue's house certain
which said, Thy daughter is dead; why
troublest thou the Master any further? As
soon as Jesus heard the word that was spoken,
he saith unto the ruler of the synagogue, Be
not afraid, only believe.—*Mark* v. 35, 36.

Let not your hearts be troubled; ye believe
in God, believe also in me. In my Father's
house are many mansions: if it were not so,
I would have told you.—*John* xiv. 1, 2.

Unto thee, O Lord, do I lift up my soul.
Turn thee unto me, and have mercy upon me;
for I am desolate and afflicted. The troubles
of my heart are enlarged. O bring thou me

out of my distress. Look upon mine afflic
tion and my pain; and forgive all my sins.—
Ps. xxv. 1, 16–18.

The Lord bless thee, and keep thee; the
Lord make his face to shine upon thee, and be
gracious unto thee; the Lord lift up his countenance upon thee, and give thee peace.—
Num. vi. 24–26.

Gracious is the Lord, and righteous, yea,
our God is merciful. I was brought low, and
he helped me. This is my comfort in my
affliction.—*Ps.* cxvi. 5—cxix. 50.

Blessed be God, even the Father of our
Lord Jesus Christ, the Father of mercies, and
the God of all comfort: who comforteth us
in all our tribulation, that we may be able to
comfort them which are in any trouble, by
the comfort wherewith we ourselves are comforted of God.—2 *Cor.* i. 3, 4.

I heard a great voice out of heaven saying,
Behold the tabernacle of God is with men.
And God shall wipe away all tears from their
eyes; and there shall be no more death,
neither sorrow nor crying, neither shall there
be any more pain. These words are true and
faithful.—*Rev.* xxi. 1–5.

The grace of our Lord Jesus Christ be with
you all. Amen.

CONSOLATION.

I.

BLESSED is the man whom thou chastenest,
O Lord, and teachest him out of thy law;
that thou mayest give him rest from the days of
adversity, until the pit be digged for the wicked. For the Lord will not cast off his people,
neither will he forsake his inheritance.—*Psalm*
xciv. 12–14.

My son, despise not the chastening of the
Lord; neither be weary of his correction: for
whom the Lord loveth he correcteth; even as a
father the son in whom he delighteth.—*Prov.*
iii. 11, 12.

Behold, happy is the man whom God correcteth: therefore despise not thou the chastening of the Almighty: for he maketh sore, and
bindeth up: he woundeth, and his hands make
whole. He shall deliver thee in six troubles:
yea, in seven there shall no evil touch thee.—
Job vi. 17–19.

There hath no temptation taken you but such
as is common to man: but God is faithful, who
will not suffer you to be tempted above that ye

are able : but will with the temptation also make
a way to escape, that ye may be able to bear
it.—1 *Cor.* x. 13.

The spirit itself beareth witness with our spirit, that we are the children of God : and if children, then heirs : heirs of God, and joint-heirs
with Christ; if so be that we suffer with him,
that we may be also glorified together. For I
reckon, that the sufferings of this present time
are not worthy to be compared with the glory
which shall be revealed in us.—*Rom.* viii.
16–18.

Beloved, think it not strange, concerning the
fiery trial which is to try you, as though some
strange thing happened unto you : but rejoice,
inasmuch as ye are partakers of Christ's sufferings : that, when his glory shall be revealed, ye
may be glad also with exceeding joy.—1 *Peter*
iv. 12, 14.

Blessed be God, even the Father of our Lord
Jesus Christ, the Father of mercies, and the
God of all comfort; who comforteth us in all
our tribulation, that we may be able to comfort
them which are in any trouble by the comfort
wherewith we ourselves are comforted of God.

For as the sufferings of Christ abound in us,
so our consolation also aboundeth by Christ.
And whether we be afflicted it is for your consolation and salvation, which is effectual in the

enduring of the same sufferings which we also suffer: or whether we be comforted, it is for your consolation and salvation. And our hope of you is steadfast, knowing, that as ye are partakers of the sufferings, so shall ye be also of the consolation.—2 *Cor.* i. 3–7.

For our light affliction, which is but for a moment, worketh for us a far more exceeding and eternal weight of glory; while we look not at the things which are seen, but at the things which are not seen : for the things which are seen are temporal; but the things that are not seen are eternal.—2 *Cor.* iv. 17, 18.

And one of the elders answered, saying unto me, What are these which are arrayed in white robes? and whence came they? And I said unto him, Sir, thou knowest. And he said to me, These are they which came out of great tribulation, and have washed their robes, and made them white in the blood of the Lamb.

Therefore are they before the throne of God, and serve him day and night in his temple: and he that sitteth on the throne shall dwell among them. They shall hunger no more, neither thirst any more; neither shall the sun light on them, nor any heat. For the Lamb which is in the midst of the throne shall feed them, and shall lead them unto living fountains of waters : and God shall wipe away all tears from their eyes.—*Rev.* vii. 13–17.

DIVINE PROTECTION.

HE that dwelleth in the secret place of the Most High, shall abide under the shadow of the Almighty. I will say of the Lord, He is my refuge and my fortress: my God: in him will I trust. Surely he shall deliver thee from the snare of the fowler, and from the noisome pestilence. He shall cover thee with his feathers, and under his wings shalt thou trust: his truth shall be thy shield and buckler.

Thou shalt not be afraid for the terror by night; nor for the arrow that flieth by day; nor for the pestilence that walketh in darkness; nor for the destruction that wasteth at noonday. A thousand shall fall at thy side, and ten thousand at thy right hand; but it shall not come nigh thee. Only with thine eyes shalt thou behold and see the reward of the wicked.— *Psalm* xci. 1–8.

Behold, happy is the man whom God correcteth; therefore despise not thou the chastening of the Almighty: for he maketh sore, and bindeth up: he woundeth, and his hands make whole. He shall deliver thee in six troubles: yea, in seven there shall no evil touch thee.

In famine he shall redeem thee from death; and in war from the power of the sword. Thou shalt be hid from the scourge of the tongue; neither shalt thou be afraid of destruction when it cometh. At destruction and famine thou shalt laugh; neither shalt thou be afraid of the beasts of the earth. For thou shalt be in league with the stones of the field; and the beasts of the field shall be at peace with thee.

And thou shalt know that thy tabernacle shall be in peace; and thou shalt visit thy habitation, and shalt not sin. Thou shalt know also that thy seed shall be great, and thine offspring as the grass of the earth. Thou shalt come to thy grave in a full age, like as a shock of corn cometh in in his season.—*Job* v. 17–26.

Because thou hast made the Lord, which is my refuge, even the Most High, thy habitation; there shall no evil befall thee, neither shall any plague come nigh thy dwelling. For he shall give his angels charge over thee, to keep thee in all thy ways. They shall bear thee up in their hands, lest thou dash thy foot against a stone.

Thou shalt tread upon the lion and adder; the young lion and the dragon shalt thou trample under foot. Because he hath set his love upon me, therefore will I deliver him: I will set him on high, because he hath known my name.— *Psalm* xci. 9–15.

TRUST IN GOD.

THE Lord is my shepherd; I shall not want. He maketh me to lie down in green pastures: he leadeth me beside the still waters. He restoreth my soul: he leadeth me in the paths of righteousness for his name's sake. Yea, though I walk through the valley of the shadow of death, I will fear no evil; for thou art with me: thy rod and thy staff they comfort me.

Thou preparest a table before me in the presence of my enemies: thou anointest my head with oil: my cup runneth over. Surely goodness and mercy shall follow me all the days of my life: and I will dwell in the house of the Lord for ever.—*Psalm* xxiii. 1–6.

The Lord is my light and my salvation; whom shall I fear? the Lord is the strength of my life; of whom shall I be afraid?—*Psalm* xxvii. 1.

The Lord is my rock, and my fortress, and my deliverer; my God, my strength, in whom I will trust; my buckler, and the horn of my salvation, and my high tower.—*Psalm* xviii. 2.

What time I am afraid, I will trust in thee.

In God I will praise his word, in God I have put my trust; I will not fear what flesh can do unto me.—*Psalm* lvi. 3, 4.

Truly my soul waiteth upon God: from him cometh my salvation. He only is my rock and my salvation; he is my defence; I shall not be greatly moved. My soul, wait thou only upon God; for my expectation is from him. He only is my rock and my salvation : he is my defence; I shall not be moved. In God is my salvation and my glory : the rock of my strength, and my refuge, is in God. Trust in him at all times; ye people, pour out your heart before him; God is a refuge for us.—*Psalm* lxii. 1, 2, 5-8.

Although the fig-tree shall not blossom, neither shall fruit be in the vines; the labor of the olive shall fail, and the fields shall yield no meat; the flock shall be cut off from the fold, and there shall be no herd in the stalls : yet I will rejoice in the Lord, I will joy in the God of my salvation. The Lord God is my strength, and he will make my feet like hind's feet, and he will make me to walk upon my high places. —*Hab.* iii. 17-19.

Behold, God is my salvation; I will trust, and not be afraid: for the Lord Jehovah is my strength and my song; he also is become my salvation.—*Isa.* xii. 2.

PENITENTS ENCOURAGED.

COME unto me, all ye that labor and are heavy laden, and I will give you rest. Take my yoke upon you, and learn of me; for I am meek and lowly in heart ; and ye shall find rest unto your souls.—*Matt.* xi. 28, 29.

Look unto me, and be ye saved, all the ends of the earth ; for I am God, and there is none else.—*Isa.* xlv. 22.

Have I any pleasure at all that the wicked should die ? saith the Lord God : and not that he should return from his ways, and live ?—*Ezek.* xviii. 22.

As I live, saith the Lord God, I have no pleasure in the death of the wicked; but that the wicked turn from his way and live: turn ye, turn ye from your evil ways ; for why will ye die, O house of Israel ?—*Ezek.* xxxiii. 10, 11.

Ho, every one that thirsteth, come ye to the waters, and he that hath no money; come ye, buy, and eat ; yea, come, buy wine and milk without money and without price.—*Isa.* lv. 1.

In the last day, that great day of the feast,

15

Jesus stood and cried, saying, If any man thirst, let him come unto me, and drink.—*John* vii. 37.

For God sent not his Son into the world to condemn the world ; but that the world through him might be saved.—*John* iii. 17.

He that spared not his own Son, but delivered him up for us all, how shall he not with him also freely give us all things ?—*Rom.* viii. 32.

For there is one God, and one mediator between God and men, the man Christ Jesus; who gave himself a ransom for all, to be testified in due time.—1 *Tim.* ii. 5, 6.

Let Israel hope in the Lord : for with the Lord there is mercy, and with him is plenteous redemption.—*Psalm* cxxx. 7.

Come now, and let us reason together, saith the Lord ; though your sins be as scarlet, they shall be as white as snow ; though they be red like crimson, they shall be as wool.—*Isa.* i. 18.

He that covereth his sins shall not prosper · but whoso confesseth and forsaketh them shall have mercy.—*Prov.* xxviii. 13.

Seek ye the Lord while he may be found, call ye upon him while he is near: let the wicked forsake his way, and the unrighteous man his thoughts: and let him return unto the Lord, and he will have mercy upon him; and to our God, for he will abundantly pardon.—*Isa.* lv. 6, 7.

Him that cometh to me I will in no wise cast out.—*John* vi. 37

Ask, and it shall be given you; seek, and ye shall find; knock, and it shall be opened unto you: for every one that asketh receiveth; and he that seeketh findeth; and to him that knocketh it shall be opened.—*Matt.* vii. 7, 8.

If thou shalt confess with thy mouth the Lord Jesus, and shalt believe in thine heart that God hath raised him from the dead, thou shalt be saved.—*Rom.* x. 9.

For all have sinned, and come short of the glory of God.—*Rom.* iii. 23.

Not by works of righteousness which we have done, but according to his mercy he saved us, by the washing of regeneration, and renewing of the Holy Ghost.—*Titus* iii. 5.

For by grace are ye saved through faith; and that not of yourselves: it is the gift of God: not of works, lest any man should boast.—*Eph.* ii. 8, 9.

He that believeth on the Son hath everlasting life.—*John* iii. 36.

Verily, verily, I say unto you, He that believeth on me hath everlasting life.—*John* vi. 47.

And he said unto them, Go ye into all the world, and preach the gospel to every creature. He that believeth and is baptized shall be saved; but he that believeth not shall be damned.—*Mark* xvi. 15, 16.

And as Moses lifted up the serpent in the

wilderness, even so must the Son of man be
lifted up: that whosoever believeth in him
should not perish, but have eternal life. For
God so loved the world, that he gave his only
begotten Son, that whosoever believeth in him
should not perish, but have everlasting life.—
John iii. 14–16.

And the Spirit and the bride say, Come.
And let him that heareth say, Come. And let
him that is athirst come. And whosoever will,
let him take the water of life freely.—*Rev*
xxii. 17.

DIVINE INVITATIONS.

HO, every one that thirsteth, come ye to the waters, and he that hath no money; come ye, buy, and eat; yea, come, buy wine and milk without money and without price. Wherefore do ye spend money for that which is not bread? and your labor for that which satisfieth not? hearken diligently unto me, and eat ye that which is good, and let your soul delight itself in fatness. Incline your ear, and come unto me; hear, and your soul shall live; and I will make an everlasting covenant with you, even the sure mercies of David.

Seek ye the Lord while he may be found, call ye upon him while he is near: let the wicked forsake his way, and the unrighteous man his thoughts: and let him return unto the Lord, and he will have mercy upon him, and to our God, for he will abundantly pardon. For my thoughts are not your thoughts, neither are your ways my ways, saith the Lord. For as the heavens are higher than the earth, so are my ways higher than your ways, and my thoughts than your thoughts.—*Isa.* li. 1-3, 6-9.

15*

And Jesus said unto them, I am the bread of life: he that cometh to me shall never hunger; and he that believeth on me shall never thirst. But I said unto you, That ye also have seen me, and believe not. All that the Father giveth me shall come to me; and him that cometh to me I will in no wise cast out. For I came down from heaven, not to do my own will, but the will of him that sent me. And this is the Father's will which hath sent me, that of all which he hath given me I should lose nothing, but should raise it up again at the last day. And this is the will of him that sent me, that every one which seeth the Son, and believeth on him, may have everlasting life: and I will raise him up at the last day.—*John* vi. 35–40.

If any man thirst, let him come unto me, and drink. He that believeth on me, as the scripture hath said, out of his belly shall flow rivers of living water.—*John* vii. 37, 38.

Come unto me, all ye that labor and are heavy laden, and I will give you rest. Take my yoke upon you, and learn of me; for I am meek and lowly in heart: and ye shall find rest unto your souls. For my yoke is easy, and my burden is light.—*Matt.* xi. 28–30.

They that be whole need not a physician, but they that are sick. But go ye and learn what that meaneth, I will have mercy, and not sacrifice: for I am not come to call the righteous, but sinners to repentance.—*Matt.* ix. 12, 13.

But seek ye first the kingdom of God, and his righteousness; and all these things shall be added unto you.—*Matt.* vi. 33.

Blessed are they which do hunger and thirst after righteousness: for they shall be filled.—*Matt.* v. 6.

And the Spirit and the bride say, Come. And let him that heareth say, Come. And let him that is athirst, come. And whosoever will, let him take the water of life freely.—*Rev.* **xxii.** **17.**

PRAYER ENJOINED.

I.

AND he spake a parable unto them to this end, that men ought always to pray, and not to faint; saying, There was in a city a judge, which feared not God, neither regarded man : and there was a widow in that city ; and she came unto him, saying, Avenge me of mine adversary. And he would not for a while: but afterward he said within himself, Though I fear not God nor regard man ; yet because this widow troubleth me, I will avenge her, lest by her continual coming she weary me.

And the Lord said, Hear what the unjust judge saith, And shall not God avenge his own elect, which cry day and night unto him, though he bear long with them ? I tell you that he will avenge them speedily. Nevertheless, when the Son of man cometh, shall he find faith on the earth ?

And he spake this parable unto certain which trusted in themselves that they were righteous, and despised others : two men went up into the temple to pray ; the one a Pharisee and the

other a publican. The Pharisee stood and prayed thus with himself, God, I thank thee, that I am not as other men are, extortioners, unjust, adulterers, or even as this publican. I fast twice in the week, I give tithes of all that I possess. And the publican, standing afar off, would not lift up so much as his eyes unto heaven, but smote upon his breast, saying, God be merciful to me a sinner. I tell you, this man went down to his house justified rather than the other : for every one that exalteth himself shall be abased, and he that humbleth himself shall be exalted.— *Luke* xviii. 1–14.

II.

And when thou prayest, thou shalt not be as the hypocrites are : for they love to pray standing in the synagogues and in the corners of the streets, that they may be seen of men. Verily I say unto you, they have their reward. But thou, when thou prayest, enter into thy closet, and when thou hast shut thy door, pray to thy Father which is in secret; and thy Father which seeth in secret shall reward thee openly. But when ye pray, use not vain repetitions, as the heathen do : for they think that they shall be heard for their much speaking. Be not ye therefore like unto them : for your Father knoweth what things ye have need of, before ye ask him.

After this manner therefore pray ye: Our Father which art in heaven, Hallowed be thy name. Thy kingdom come. Thy will be done in earth as it is in heaven. Give us this day our daily bread. And forgive us our debts, as we forgive our debtors. And lead us not unto temptation, but deliver us from evil. For thine is the kingdom, and the power, and the glory, for ever. Amen.

For if ye forgive men their trespasses, your heavenly Father will also forgive you: but if ye forgive not men their trespasses, neither will your Father forgive your trespasses.— *Matt.* vi. 5–15.

Verily, verily, I say unto you, Whatsoever ye shall ask the Father in my name, he will give it you. Hitherto have ye asked nothing in my name: ask, and ye shall receive, that your joy may be full.—*John* xvi. 23, 24.

Again I say unto you, That if two of you shall agree on earth as touching any thing that they shall ask, it shall be done for them of my Father which is in heaven. For where two or three are gathered together in my name, there am I in the midst of them.—*Matt.* xviii. 19, 20.

PRAYER ENCOURAGED.

BUT if from thence thou shalt seek the Lord thy God, thou shalt find him, if thou seek him with all thine heart, and with all thy soul. When thou art in tribulation, and all these things are come upon thee, even in the latter days, if thou turn to the Lord thy God, and shalt be obedient unto his voice; (for the Lord thy God is a merciful God;) he will not forsake thee, neither destroy thee, nor forget the covenant of thy fathers, which he sware unto them —*Deut.* iv. 29–31.

If I shut up heaven that there be no rain, or if I command the locusts to devour the land, or if I send pestilence among my people; if my people which are called by my name, shall humble themselves, and pray, and seek my face, and turn from their wicked ways; then will I hear from heaven, and will forgive their sin, and will heal their land.—2 *Chron.* vii. 13, 14.

And call upon me in the day of trouble: I will deliver thee, and thou shalt glorify me.— *Psalm* l. 15.

And it shall come to pass, that before they call, I will answer; and while they are yet speaking, I will hear.—*Isa.* lxv. 24.

And I say unto you, Ask, and it shall be given you; seek, and ye shall find; knock, and it shall be opened unto you. For every one that asketh, receiveth; and he that seeketh findeth; and to him that knocketh, it shall be opened. If a son shall ask bread of any of you that is a father, will he give him a stone? or if he ask a fish, will he for a fish give him a serpent? or if he shall ask an egg, will he offer him a scorpion? If ye then, being evil, know how to give good gifts unto your children; how much more shall your heavenly Father give the Holy Spirit to them that ask him?—*Luke* xi. 9–13.

And this is the confidence that we have in him, that if we ask any thing according to his will, he heareth us: and if we know that he hear us, whatsoever we ask, we know that we have the petitions that we desired of him.—1 *John* v. 14, 15.

Let us therefore come boldly unto the throne of grace that we may obtain mercy, and **find grace** to help in time of need.—*Heb.* vi. 16.

BENEDICTIONS.

TO God only wise, be glory through Jesus Christ for ever. Amen.—*Rom.* xvi. 27.

Grace be unto you, and peace, from God our Father, and from the Lord Jesus Christ.—1 *Cor.* i. 3.

The grace of the Lord Jesus Christ, and the love of God, and the communion of the Holy Ghost, be with you all. Amen.—2 *Cor.* xiii. 14.

Brethren, the grace of our Lord Jesus Christ be with your spirit. Amen.—*Gal.* vi. 18.

Peace be to the brethren, and love with faith, from God the Father and Lord Jesus Christ. Grace be with all them that love our Lord Jesus Christ in sincerity. Amen.—*Eph.* vi. 23, 24.

The peace of God which passeth all understanding, shall keep your hearts and minds through Christ Jesus. Now unto God and our Father be glory for ever and ever. Amen.— *Phil.* iv. 7, 20.

Grace, mercy, and peace, from God the Father and Christ Jesus our Lord.—2 *Tim.* i. 2.

Grace to you, and peace, from God our Father and the Lord Jesus Christ.—*Phil.* 3.

16

Now the God of peace, that brought again from the dead our Lord Jesus, that great shepherd of the sheep, through the blood of the everlasting covenant, make you perfect in every good work to do his will, working in you that which is well-pleasing in his sight, through Jesus Christ; to whom be glory for ever and ever. Amen.—*Heb.* xiii. 20, 21.

Grace and peace be multiplied unto you through the knowledge of God, and of Jesus our Lord.—2 *Peter* ii. 2.

Grace be with you, mercy, and peace, from God the Father, and from the Lord Jesus Christ, the Son of the Father, in truth and love.—2 *John* ii. 3.

Now unto him that is able to keep you from falling, and to present you faultless before the presence of his glory with exceeding joy, to the only wise God our Saviour, be glory and majesty, dominion and power, both now and ever. Amen.—*Jude* 24, 25.

The grace of our Lord Jesus Christ be with you all. Amen.—*Rev.* xxii. 21.

THE

Burial Service,

WITH

SUGGESTIVE THOUGHTS

FOR

FUNERAL OCCASIONS.

THE EPISCOPAL

BURIAL SERVICE.

¶ *The Minister, meeting the Corpse at the entrance of the Churchyard and going before it, either into the Church, or towards the Grave, shall say, or sing,*

I AM the resurrection and the life, saith the Lord: he that believeth in me, though he were dead, yet shall he live : and whosoever liveth and believeth in me, shall never die.— *John* xi. 25, 26.

I KNOW that my Redeemer liveth, and that he shall stand at the latter day upon the earth. And though after my skin worms destroy this body, yet in my flesh shall I see God : whom I shall see for myself, and mine eyes shall behold, and not another.—*Job* xix. 25, 26, 27.

WE brought nothing into this world, and it is certain we can carry nothing out. The Lord gave, and the Lord hath taken away, blessed be the Name of the Lord.—1 *Tim.* vi. 7; *Job* i. 21.

16*

¶ *After they are come into the Church, shall be said or sung the fol lowing Anthem, taken from the 39th and 90th Psalms.*

LORD, let me know my end, and the number of my days; that I may be certified how long I have to live.

Behold, thou hast made my days as it were a span long, and mine age is even as nothing in respect of thee; and verily every man living is altogether vanity.

For man walketh in a vain shadow, and disquieteth himself in vain; he heapeth up riches, and cannot tell who shall gather them.

And now, Lord, what is my hope? Truly my hope is even in thee.

Deliver me from all mine offences; and make me not a rebuke unto the foolish.

When thou with rebukes dost chasten man for sin, thou makest his beauty to consume away, like as it were a moth fretting a garment: every man therefore is but vanity.

Hear my prayer, O Lord, and with thine ears consider my calling; hold not thy peace at my tears:

For I am a stranger with thee, and a sojourner, as all my fathers were.

O spare me a little, that I may recover my strength, before I go hence and be no more seen.

Lord, thou hast been our refuge, from one generation to another.

Before the mountains were brought forth, or ever the earth and the world were made, thou art God from everlasting, and world without end.

Thou turnest man to destruction; again thou sayest, Come again, ye children of men.

For a thousand years in thy sight are but as yesterday; seeing that is past as a watch in the night.

As soon as thou scatterest them they are even as a sleep; and fade away suddenly like the grass.

In the morning it is green, and groweth up; but in the evening it is cut down, dried up, and withered.

For we consume away in thy displeasure; and are afraid at thy wrathful indignation.

Thou hast set our misdeeds before thee; and our secret sins in the light of thy countenance.

For when thou art angry, all our days are gone; we bring our years to an end, as it were a tale that is told.

The days of our age are threescore years and ten; and though men be so strong that they come to fourscore years, yet is their strength then but labor and sorrow; so soon passeth it away, and we are gone.

So teach us to number our days, that we may apply our hearts unto wisdom.

Glory be to the Father, and to the Son, and to the Holy Ghost ;

As it was in the beginning, is now, and ever shall be, world without end. Amen.

¶ *Then shall follow the Lesson, taken out of the Fifteenth Chapter of the first Epistle of St. Paul to the Corinthians.*

1 *Cor.* xv. 20.

NOW is Christ risen from the dead, and become the first-fruits of them that slept. For since by man came death, by man came also the resurrection of the dead. For as in Adam all die, even so in Christ shall all be made alive. But every man in his own order : Christ the first-fruits ; afterwards they that are Christ's, at his coming. Then cometh the end, when he shall have delivered up the Kingdom to God, even the Father ; when he shall have put down all rule and all authority, and power. For he must reign, till he hath put all enemies under his feet. The last enemy that shall be destroyed is death. For he hath put all things under his feet. But when he saith, all things are put under him, it is manifest that he is excepted, which did put all things under him. And when all things shall be subdued unto him, then shall the Son also himself be subject unto Him that put all things under him, that God may be all in all.

Else what shall they do which are baptized for the dead, if the dead rise not at all? Why are they then baptized for the dead? and why stand we in jeopardy every hour? I protest by your rejoicing, which I have in Christ Jesus our Lord, I die daily. If after the manner of men I have fought with beasts at Ephesus, what advantageth it me, if the dead rise not? let us eat and drink, for to-morrow we die. Be not deceived: evil communications corrupt good manners. Awake to righteousness, and sin not; for some have not the knowledge of God. I speak this to your shame.

But some man will say, How are the dead raised up? and with what body do they come? Thou fool! that which thou sowest is not quickened, except it die. And that which thou sowest, thou sowest not that body that shall be, but bare grain, it may chance of wheat, or of some other grain. But God giveth it a body as it hath pleased him, and to every seed his own body. All flesh is not the same flesh; but there is one kind of flesh of men, another flesh of beasts, another of fishes, and another of birds. There are also celestial bodies, and bodies terrestrial; but the glory of the celestial is one, and the glory of the terrestial is another. There is one glory of the sun, and another glory of the moon, and another glory of the stars; for one star differeth from another star in glory.

So also is the resurrection of the dead. It is sown in corruption; it is raised in incorruption: it is sown in dishonour; it is raised in glory: it is sown in weakness; it is raised in power: it is sown a natural body; it is raised a spiritual body. There is a natural body, and there is a spiritual body. And so it is written, The first man Adam was made a living soul; the last Adam was made a quickening spirit. Howbeit, that was not first which is spiritual, but that which is natural; and afterwards that which is spiritual. The first man is of the earth, earthy: the second man is the Lord from heaven. As is the earthy, such are they that are earthy: and as is the heavenly, such are they also that are heavenly. And as we have borne the image of the earthy, we shall also bear the image of the heavenly.

Now this I say, brethren, that flesh and blood cannot inherit the Kingdom of God; neither doth corruption inherit incorruption. Behold, I show you a mystery: we shall not all sleep, but we shall all be changed, in a moment, in the twinkling of an eye, at the last trump: for the trumpet shall sound, and the dead shall be

raised incorruptible, and we shall be changed
For this corruptible must put on incorruption,
and this mortal must put on immortality.

So when this corruptible shall have put on
incorruption, and this mortal shall have put on
immortality; then shall be brought to pass the
saying that is written, Death is swallowed up
in victory. O death, where is thy sting? O
grave, where is thy victory? The sting of
death is sin; and the strength of sin is the Law.
But thanks be to God, which giveth us the victory through our Lord Jesus Christ. Therefore,
my beloved brethren, be ye steadfast, unmov-
able, always abounding in the work of the Lord,
forasmuch as ye know that your labor is not
in vain in the Lord.

*¶ When they come to the grave, while the Corpse is made ready to be
laid into the earth, shall be sung or said,*

MAN, that is born of a woman, hath but a
short time to live, and is full of misery.
He cometh up, and is cut down, like a flower;
he fleeth as it were a shadow, and never continueth in one stay.

In the midst of life we are in death: of whom
may we seek for succor, but of thee, O Lord,
who for our sins art justly displeased?

Yet, O Lord God most holy, O Lord most

mighty, O holy and most merciful **Saviour, de-**
liver us not into the bitter pains of eternal death

Thou knowest, Lord, the secrets of our hearts;
shut not thy merciful ears to our prayer; but
spare us, Lord most holy, O God most mighty,
O holy and merciful Saviour, thou most worthy
Judge eternal, suffer us not, at our last hour, for
any pains of death, to fall from thee.

¶ *Then, while the earth shall be cast upon the Body by some **standing**
by, the Minister shall say,*

FORASMUCH as it hath pleased Almighty
God, in his wise providence, to take out of
this world the soul of our deceased *brother,** we
therefore commit *his* body to the ground; earth
to earth, ashes to ashes, dust to dust; looking
for the general Resurrection in the last day,
and the life of the world to come, through our
Lord Jesus Christ; at whose second coming in
glorious majesty to judge the world, the earth
and the sea shall give up their dead; and the
corruptible bodies of those who sleep in him
shall be changed, and made like unto his own
glorious body; according to the mighty working whereby he is able to subdue all things
unto himself.

*Or sister, or friend.

¶ *Then shall be said, or sung,*

I HEARD a voice from heaven, saying unto me, Write, From henceforth blessed are the dead who die in the Lord: even so saith the Spirit; for they rest from their labors.—*Rev.* xiv. 13.

¶ *Then the Minister shall say the Lord's Prayer :*

OUR FATHER, who art in heaven, Hallowed be thy Name. Thy kingdom come. Thy will be done on earth, As it is in heaven. Give us this day our daily bread. And forgive us our trespasses, As we forgive those who trespass against us. And lead us not into temptation; But deliver us from evil. Amen.

¶ *Then the Minister shall say one or both of the following prayers, at his discretion.*

ALMIGHTY GOD, with whom do live the spirits of those who depart hence in the Lord, and with whom the souls of the faithful, after they are delivered from the burden of the flesh, are in joy and felicity; We give thee hearty thanks for the good examples of all those thy servants, who, having finished their course in faith, do now rest from their labors. And we beseech thee, that we, with all those who

17

are departed in the true faith of thy holy **Name**, may have our perfect consummation and bliss, both in body and soul, in thy eternal and everlasting glory; through Jesus Christ our Lord. *Amen.*

O MERCIFUL GOD, the Father of our Lord Jesus Christ, who is the resurrection and the life; in whom whosoever believeth, shall live, though he die; and whosoever liveth, and believeth in him, shall not die eternally; who also hath taught us, by his holy Apostle Saint Paul, not to be sorry, as men without hope, for those who sleep in him; We humbly beseech thee, O Father, to raise us from the death of sin unto the life of righteousness; that, when we shall depart this life, we may rest in him; and that, at the general Resurrection in the last day, we may be found acceptable in thy sight; and receive that blessing, which thy well-beloved Son shall then pronounce to all who love and fear thee, saying, Come, ye blessed children of my Father, receive the kingdom prepared for you from the beginning of the world. Grant this, we beseech thee, O merciful Father, through Jesus Christ, our Mediator and Redeemer. *Amen.*

THE grace of our Lord Jesus Christ, **and the** love of God, and fellowship of the **Holy** Ghost, be with us all evermore. *Amen.*

SUGGESTIVE THOUGHTS.

ATTENDANCE at funerals constitutes a constantly recurring claim upon the time and thought of clergymen. They are frequently called on at short notice, and often when pressed with other duties. Aside from the remarks which the peculiar circumstances of each case may call forth, it is desirable they should address some instruction to those present, other than the relatives; some of whom seldom attend any other religious services. The following suggestions are not intended to serve as plans for sermons, but as simply opening lines of thought, where other and more mature preparation cannot well be made.

LORD, make me to know my end, and the measure of my days, what it is; that I may know how frail I am.—*Ps.* xxxix. 4.

1. The frailty and brevity of human life impressed. 2. The end of life should be kept in view, to shape its conduct. 3. Divine aid is implored, that this important but difficult lesson may be learned.

Let it lead to humiliation, and prayer for assistance.

In the morning it flourisheth and groweth up; in the evening it is cut down and withereth.—*Ps.* xc. 6.

Life's rapid transitions; extremes, as within a single day. 1. In the morning, its beauty, vigor, promise. 2. In the evening, withered as to its glory, cut off from its connections, removed from its sphere.

But purity and truth shall survive the body's death.

Lover and friend hast thou put far from me, and mine acquaintance into darkness.—*Ps.* lxxxviii 18.

1. As friendship and kinship constitute one of the chief sources of human happiness, so their dissolution by death forms one of the chief elements of human sorrow. 2. It is God who causes, or permits these events; first, by the natural constitution of our being; second, by the control of His providence. A friend has done it.

Let it draw us to Him. He will sustain.

So when this corruptible shall have put on incorruption, and this mortal shall have put on immortality, then shall be brought to pass the saying that is written, Death is swallowed up in victory.—1 *Cor.* xv. 54.

The triumph of the saints over death, and the redemption, even of their bodies, from its power, through the resurrection of Christ from the dead. 1. The corruptible shall put on incorruption. No more decay. 2. The mortal shall put on immortality. No more death. 3. Glorious victory.

I would not have you to be ignorant, brethren, concerning them which are asleep; that ye sorrow not, even as others which have no hope.—*Thess.* iv. 13.

Glorious hope, and great consolation concerning them which sleep in Jesus. Read what follows. Christ shall bring them with Him in glory, when He comes. What a change!

For our conversation is in heaven; from whence also, we look for the Saviour, the Lord Jesus Christ; who shall change our vile body, that it may be fashioned like unto his glorious body.—*Phil.* iii. 20, 21.

A marvelous transformation. 1. Christ shall change the vile body! 2. He shall fashion it like to His own glorious body.

Changed to youth, beauty, vigor, glory, immortality. Still more glorious shall the spirit be.

And as we have borne the image of the earthy, we shall also bear the image of the heavenly.—1 *Cor.* xv. 49.

A wonderful contrast for the saints, in the resurrection and glorification of the body. 1. It is sown in corruption, and raised in incorruption. 2. It is sown in dishonor, and raised in glory. 3. It is sown in weakness, and raised in power. 4. It is sown a natural body, and raised a spiritual body.

Eye hath not seen, nor ear heard, neither have entered into the heart of man, the things which God hath prepared for them that love him. But God hath revealed them unto us by his Spirit.—1 *Cor.* ii. 9, 10.

1. God loves them, who love Him. 2. His love is not in word only. He has prepared great and good things for them. 3. These great and good things transcend all earthly and sensible standards. 4. To their verity, however, the Spirit certifies, in the hearts of the inheritors.

I go to prepare a place for you.—*John* xiv. 2.

1. Christ, though absent from His disciples, is still mindful of them. 2. He is engaged on their behalf, preparing a place for their reception and habitation.

This is their comfort in the house of their pilgrimage.

Come, ye blessed of my Father, inherit the kingdom prepared for you from the foundation of the world.—*Matt.* xxv. 34.

Life and earth, and sin and sorrow, end to the people of God, with a joyous welcome to a kingly heritage. 1. Christ's followers are the blessed of the Father. 2. They will not simply dwell in a kingly realm, but inherit one. 3. This is a fixed and long settled preparation for them.

Blessed are the dead which die in the Lord from henceforth : Yea, saith the Spirit, that they may rest from their labors, and their works do follow them.— *Rev.* xiv. 13.

1. Death cannot hinder, but hastens the blessedness of the saints of God. 2. They rest from all toil, pain, trial and distress. 3. Their works appear with them, not to claim reward, but to magnify grace.

These are they which came out of great tribulation, and have washed their robes, and made them white in the blood of the Lamb.—*Rev.* vii. 14.

The goodly company of the redeemed in heaven. 1. They came out of great tribulation. Gold tried in the fire. 2. They were purified and glorified through the blood of the Lamb. No other way to heavenly joy and bliss.

They shall hunger no more, neither thirst any more; neither shall the sun light on them, nor any heat.—*Rev.* vii. 16.

The blissful estate of the glorified in heaven. 1. No more exposure to evil from bodily conditions, hunger, thirst, sickness. death. 2. No more exposure to calamities arising from tne external conditions of life, as sunstroke, heat, or other outward misfortunes.

And God shall wipe away all tears from their eyes.—*Rev.* vii. 17.

1. Tears, the symbol of all human sorrow and suffering, shall not be known in heaven. 2. On earth a mingled cup of smiles and tears, of joys and sorrows. 3. In the perdition of the ungodly, tears never cease. There is weeping, and wailing, and gnashing of teeth. There is a calm for those who weep.

And God shall wipe away all tears from their eyes; and there shall be no more death, neither sorrow, nor crying : neither shall there be any more pain ; for the former things are passed away.—*Rev.* xxi. 4.

1. A complete deliverance from all earthly ills, which ills these things represent. 2. God wipes away the tears, and secures this bliss. His love prompts it ; His purpose determines it ; His power secures it.

And there shall be no night there ; and they need no candle, neither light of the sun ; for the Lord God giveth them light : and they shall reign forever and ever.—*Rev.* xxii. 5.

The bliss of the righteous typified in the life to come.

1. Night indicates the passing of days, and the march of wasting years. Eternity, not time, there. 2. Night implies exhaustion and weariness, and brings a season of rest. No exhaustion or weariness there. 3. Night and darkness are emblems of evil, and the opportunity for iniquity and crime. None there.

God himself shall constitute their inexhaustible supply of bliss, and their eternal life shall be a kingly reign.

My son, despise not thou the chastening of the Lord, nor faint when thou art rebuked of him. For whom the Lord loveth he chasteneth, and scourgeth every son whom he receiveth.—*Heb.* xii. 5, 6.

1. Providential trials are the discipline which a kind Father sends upon the children of His love. 2. The end and purpose of them, is, to purify and sanctify those who endure them, and fit them for a better life.

It is God's way of dealing with His children.

For our light affliction, which is but for a moment, worketh for us a far more exceeding and eternal weight of glory.—2 *Cor.* iv. 17.

1. Thus God works eternal fruits of joy, from earthly seeds of sorrow. 2. But this is true only to those who receive the light afflictions graciously, looking at the things which are unseen, but eternal.

The "light afflictions," and the "weight of glory," are put in contrast. So are the "moment" of endurance, and the "eternal" enjoyment.

What an inspiration for suffering saints!

I know, O Lord, that thy judgments are right, and that thou in faithfulness hast afflicted me. Let, I pray thee, thy merciful kindness be for my comfort, according to thy word unto thy servant.—*Ps.* cxix. 75, 76.

1. God's judgments are right; needed. 2. His afflictions spring from His fatherly faithfulness to His creatures. 3. His merciful kindness invoked, for comfort and support.

Yea, though I walk through the valley of the shadow of death, I will fear no evil: for thou art with me; thy rod and thy staff they comfort me.—*Ps.* xxiii. 4.

Triumphant trust in God, in the most trying conditions. His presence cheers, His power sustains.

Jesus said, Suffer little children, and forbid them not, to come unto me; for of such is the kingdom of heaven.—*Matt.* xix. 14.

1. The love of Jesus for little children exhibited. 2. He still calls them to himself, in the mansions above. They are in the most blissful of homes, and objects of the most perfect love.

And he took them up in his arms, put his hands upon them, and blessed them.—*Mark* x. 14

1. The gentle affection of Jesus for little children. Nor is His love less now than then. 2. He blessed them. So He does still, even by calling them to Himself.

They are the lambs of the Good Shepherd's flock.

But now he is dead, wherefore should I fast? Can I bring him back again? I shall go to him, but he shall not return to me.—*2 Sam.* xii. 23.

1. Unreasonable grief in bereavement restrained. 2. A re-union with the dead in this life impossible. 3. A reunion with the departed in the future possible, and more blessed than if it could be realized on earth.

And all wept and bewailed her; but he said, Weep not; she is not dead, but sleepeth.—*Luke* viii. 52.

Narrate the circumstances of this case.

1. The young die, as well as the old. 2. The presence of Jesus brings joy to the most sorrowful heart and home. 3. Christ is the resurrection and the life. He can make the dead to live. 4. He has full sympathy with, and compassion for the grief of afflicted parents and friends.

Mark the perfect man, and behold the upright; for the end of that man is peace.—*Ps.* xxxvii. 37.

1. A good man stands in the world, as a monument to be observed; commanding attention, and moulding by his silent influence. 2. The end of life, rather than any of its preceding stages, reveals its character, and is the test of its quality. 3. The end of the good, is peace. Peace in view both of the past and the future. Even where it is not rapturous delight, it is serene confidence.

A good life only, can bring a peaceful end.

For I know that thou wilt bring me to death, and to the house appointed for all living.—*Job* **xxx.** 23.

Do not let our interest in the loss and affliction of others, cause us to forget our personal relation to death and eternity.

1. God will bring *me* to death: each one of us. What comes to others, comes to us. The lessons are to the living, not to the dead. 2. And this we positively know. From the course of nature; from the word of God; from universal observation. Are we prepared for the event?

For what is your life? It is even a vapour that appeareth for a little time, and then vanisheth away.— *James* iv. 14.

So frail and ephemeral is life—is *our* life. Why then do we, 1. Trust it so confidently? 2. Spend it so lavishly? 3. Neglect it so heedlessly?

The Lord maketh sore, and bindeth up; he woundeth, and his hands make whole.—*Job* v. 18.

1. God is to be recognized in all the afflictions of life. This both dignifies and sanctifies sorrow. 2. He who afflicts can comfort; He who wounds can heal. Out of trial may come consolation.

For we know that if our earthly house of this tabernacle were dissolved, we have a building of God, a house not made with hands, eternal in the heavens.— 2 *Cor.* v. 1.

The present and the future of the righteous, contrasted. 1. Here the soul occupies an earthly house, a frail tent, dissolving and perishable. 2. There it will be a building of God, made without hands, in the heavens, and eternal.

The death of the saint is a victory, not a defeat.

FORMS

OF

MARRIAGE SERVICE,

AS USED BY

VARIOUS CLERGYMEN,

INCLUDING THE

EPISCOPAL MARRIAGE SERVICE.

.

FORMS OF MARRIAGE SERVICE.

EACH clergyman will exercise his own choice, both as to the form by which he will solemnize the bans, and also as to those exercises which precede or follow the formal marriage service. Some precede the marriage with reading appropriate Scripture selections, remarks, and prayer. Some omit one or all of these at the beginning, and add remarks and prayer at the conclusion. Some offer prayer both before and after the service. Each one will be governed by his own sense of propriety in the case.

The following forms may constitute suggestive helps, even where neither of them may be used entire.

I.*

The parties standing before the minister, the man at the woman's right hand, and after prayer, or such other exercises as may be had, the minister shall say:

IF it be your intention to take each other as husband and wife, you will manifest it by uniting your right hands.

This being done, he shall say to the man,

YOU now take this woman, whose hand you hold, to be your lawful wedded wife. Do you solemnly promise, before God and these witnesses, that you will love, honor and cherish her; and that, forsaking all others for her alone, you will faithfully

---

* This Form of service was furnished, for insertion in this work, by a pastor who has long used it.

18

perform to her all the duties which a **husband owes** to a wife, so long as you both shall live ?

He answers, I do. *Then to the woman,*

YOU now take this man whose hand you hold, to be your lawful wedded husband. Do you solemnly promise, before God and these witnesses, that you will love, honor and cherish him ; and that, forsaking all others for him alone, you will faithfully perform to him all the duties which a wife owes to a husband, so long as you both shall live ?

She answers, I do. *Then, if a ring be used, the minister shall take it from the man, and say to him,*

AND this ring you give to her whom you have now taken as your lawful wife, in token of the affection with which you will cherish her, and the fidelity with which you will perform the sacred vows you have now made ?

He answers, I do. *Then to her,*

AND this ring you accept from him whom you have now taken as your lawful husband, and will wear as a sign and evidence of your affection for him, and the fidelity with which you will discharge your duties as a wife ?

She answers, I do. *He then returns the ring to the man, directing him to place it on the hand of the woman. After which he says :*

LET this be the seal of your plighted faith, and of your mutual affection and fidelity ; a memorial

of this sacred service, and of the holy bonds of marriage, by which you are bound henceforth till death
shall separate you.

A S you have thus solemnly agreed before God
and these witnesses, I pronounce you lawfully married husband and wife. May Divine favor
crown this union and your future lives, with all temporal and spiritual blessings in Christ Jesus our Saviour, and bring you to the life everlasting. Amen.

II.*

The parties standing before the minister, he shall say,

D IVINE Revelation has declared marriage to be
honorable in all. It is an institution of God, ordained in the time of man's innocency, before he had
sinned against his Maker, and been yet banished
from Paradise. It was given in wisdom and in kindness, to repress irregular affection, to support social
order, and to provide that, through well-ordered
families, truth and holiness might be transmitted from
one age to another. Earlier, therefore, than all laws
of merely human origin, it lies at the basis of all
human legislation and civil government, and the
peace and well-being of the nation and land.

We learn from the history of our Saviour, that He
honored a marriage festival with His presence, and

---

* This Form was furnished by REV. WM. R. WILLIAMS, D.D., of
New York City; and is the one which he has himself used for many
years.

wrought there the beginning of His miracles. And by His Holy Spirit, speaking through His apostle, He has selected the union thus formed, as an apt emblem of the union, endeared and indissoluble, that binds together Himself and His own ransomed Church.

A relation that is thus consecrated, should not be formed thoughtlessly and irreverently; but advisedly in the fear of God, and as for the purposes for which He, its Divine Author, ordained and blessed matrimony.

And now, as in His sight, **and as you will answer** in the day when all hearts shall be made manifest, I charge you to declare if there be any cause that should prevent your lawful union.

From your silence, I presume that there is none. Will the parties now join their right hands ?

Then he shall say to the man,

DO you, *A. B.*, take *C. D.*, whom you now hold by the hand, as your true and lawful Wife; and, God helping you, will you love, cherish, honor and protect her, cleaving only and ever unto her, until God by death shall separate you ?

He shall answer, I do.   Then to the woman,

DO you, *C. D.*, take *A. B.*, whom you now hold by the hand, as your true and lawful Husband;

and, God helping you, will you love, cherish, honor and obey him, cleaving only and ever unto him, until God by death shall separate you?

She shall answer, I do.

Where a ring is used, the Groom is here to place it on the Bride's hand; the minister adds these words,

THE circle, the emblem of eternity; and gold, the type of what is least tarnished and most enduring;—it is to show how lasting and imperishable the faith now mutually pledged.

As the union now formed is to be sundered only by death, it becomes you to consider the duties you solemnly assume. If these be remembered and faithfully discharged, they will add to the happiness of this life, lightening by dividing its inevitable sorrows, and heightening by doubling all its blessedness. But if these obligations be neglected and violated, you cannot escape the keenest misery, as well as the darkest guilt.

It is the duty of the Husband to provide for the support of his Wife, to shelter her from danger, and to cherish for her a manly and unalterable affection, it being the command of God's word, that husbands love their wives, even as Christ loved the Church, and gave His own life for her.

It is the duty of the Wife to reverence and obey her Husband, and to put on the ornament of a meek and quiet spirit, which is, in God's sight, an ornament of great price, His word commanding that Wives be subject unto their own Husbands, even as the Church is subject unto Christ.

It is the duty of both to delight each in the society of the other; to remember that, in interest and in reputation as in affection, they are to be henceforth one and undivided; to preserve an inviolable fidelity, and to see to it, that what God has joined thus together, man never puts asunder.

PRAYER.

OUR Father, who art in Heaven, who hast, in thy wise and tender care for mankind, ordained and blessed the institution of matrimony, we pray of Thee, graciously to regard Thy servant and hand-maiden, who have thus solemnly pledged themselves to each other, and sworn unto Thee; that, through Thy good care and guidance, they may evermore remember and keep these their vows; be kept themselves in unbroken concord and sympathy all the days of their earthly life; and be at the last, with all those most near and most dear unto them, gathered an unbroken household to Thy right hand on the day of judgment. And may all of us, here assembled, be of that blessed company who shall be called to go in to the Marriage Supper of the Lamb. And this we ask, only in the name and through the merits of Him, Thine own Son and our Redeemer, the Lord Jesus Christ. Amen.

BENEDICTION.

In pursuance of your solemn pledges thus given and in the name of the Father, the Son and the Holy

Ghost, I pronounce you Husband and Wife: and may the God before whom you have thus vowed, look upon you, to make you blessed and a blessing, in all your earthly ways; and grant you, when the snares and trials of this life are ended, a glad and eternal reunion in heaven. Amen.

III.*

The parties standing before the minister, he shall say:

MARRIAGE is a joyous occasion. It is connected in our thoughts with the magic charm of home, and with all that is pleasant and attractive in the tenderest and most sacred relations of life. When celebrated in Cana of Galilee, it was sanctioned and cheered by the presence of the Lord himself; and is declared by an inspired Apostle, to be honorable in all.

AND now, if you A. B. and C. D. have at present appeared for the purpose of being joined in legal wedlock, you will please to signify this intention, by uniting your right hands.

The minister shall then say to the man,

A., DO you take the lady whom you now hold by the hand, to be your lawful and wedded wife ?

Answer, I do; or, assent.

---

* This Form was furnished by the REV. ROLLIN H. NEAL, D.D., of Boston, being the one used by him during his long ministry.

DO you promise to love and cherish her, in sickness and in health, for richer for poorer, for
better for worse, and forsaking all others keep thee
only unto her, so long as you both shall live?

Answer, I do ; *or assent. Then to the woman,*

O., DO you take the gentleman who now stands
by your side and who holds you by the
hand, to be your lawful and wedded husband?

Answer, I do ; *or assent.*

DO you promise, to love and cherish him, in sickness and in health, for richer for poorer, for
better for worse, and forsaking all others, keep thee
only unto him, so long as you both shall live?

Answer, I do ; *or assent.*

YOU mutually promise in the presence of God
and of these witnesses, that you will at all
times and in all circumstances, conduct yourselves
toward one another as becometh Husband and Wife?

Both answer, I do; *or assent.*

THAT you will love, cherish and adhere to one
another, until separated by death?

Both answer, I do ; *or assent. If a ring be used, the minister will
say to the Bridegroom,*

YOU will please place this ring on the hand of
your affianced Bride. . . . . And reunite your
hands.

He shall continue :

HAVING taken these pledges of your affection and vows of fidelity, I do therefore, by authority of the laws of this State, sanctioned by divine authority, pronounce you, A. B. and C. D., lawfully married, Husband and Wife; in the name of the Father, and of the Son, and of the Holy Ghost. Amen.

WHAT, therefore, God hath joined together, let not man put asunder.

PRAYER.

IV.*

The parties standing before the minister, he shall say :

DEARLY beloved: We are gathered together here in the sight of God, and in the face of this company, to join together this Man and this Woman in holy matrimony, which is commended of St. Paul to be honorable among all men ; and therefore is not by any to be entered into unadvisedly or lightly; but reverently, discreetly, advisedly, and in the fear of God. Into this holy estate, these two persons present come now to be joined. If any man

---

* This abridged Form of Episcopal Marriage Service is from DR. HIRAM MATTISON's *Pocket Manual.*

can show just cause why they may not lawfully be
joined together, let him now speak, or else hereafter
forever hold his peace.

If no impediment shall be alleged, the minister shall say to the man,

M., WILT thou have this Woman to thy wedded wife, to live together after God's ordinance, in the holy estate of matrimony?   Wilt thou
love her, comfort her, honor, and keep her, in sickness and in health; and, forsaking all others, keep
thee only unto her, so long as ye both shall live?

The man shall answer, I will.

Then shall the minister say to the woman,

N., WILT thou have this Man to thy wedded
husband, to live together after God's ordinance, in the holy estate of matrimony?   Wilt
thou obey him and serve him, love, honor, and keep
him, in sickness and in health; and, forsaking all
others, keep thee only unto him, so long as ye both
shall live?

The woman shall answer, I will.

*Then shall the man give unto the woman a ring.   And the minister,
taking the ring, shall deliver it unto the man, to put it upon
the fourth finger of the woman's left hand.   And the man, holding the ring there, and taught by the minister, shall say :*

WITH this ring I thee wed, and with all my
worldly goods I thee endow: In the name of
the Father, and of the Son, and of the Holy Ghost.
Amen.

Or, if the candidate prefer not to repeat this portion of the service,
the minister may use in its place the following :

AS a token and seal of this covenant, you will now give and receive the marriage ring, and join your right hands.

THOSE whom God hath joined together, let no man put asunder.

Then shall the minister speak unto the company :

FORASMUCH as *M.* and *N.* have consented together in holy wedlock, and have witnessed the same before God and this company, and thereto have pledged their faith, each to the other, by giving and receiving a ring, and by joining their hands; I pronounce them Husband and Wife together, in the name of the Father, and of the Son, and of the Holy Ghost. Amen.

PRAYER.

V.*

THE EPISCOPAL MARRIAGE SERVICE.

*At the day and time appointed for Solemnization of Matrimony, the
persons to be married shall come into the body of the church, or
shall be ready in some proper house, with their friends and
neighbors; and there standing together, the Man on the right
hand, and the Woman on the left the minister shall say:*

DEARLY beloved: We are gathered together
here in the sight of God, and in the face of
this company, to join together this Man and this
Woman in holy matrimony; which is commended of
St. Paul to be honorable among all men: and therefore is not by any to be entered into unadvisedly or
lightly; but reverently, discreetly, advisedly, and in
the fear of God. Into this holy estate, these two persons present come now to be joined. If any man can
show just cause why they may not lawfully be joined
together, let him now speak, or else hereafter forever
hold his peace.

---

* The Service here given is that now in use in the Protestant Episcopal Church in this country, as found in the Book of Common
Prayer, and is inserted here for the convenience of those who may
have occasion to use it, in whole, or in part.

And, also, speaking unto the persons who are to be married, he shall say :

I REQUIRE and charge you both, as ye will an swer at the dreadful day of judgment, when the secrets of all hearts shall be disclosed, that if either of you know any impediment why ye may not be lawfully joined together in matrimony, ye do now confess it. For be ye well assured, that if any persons are joined together otherwise than as God's word doth allow, their marriage is not lawful.

If no impediment shall be alleged, the minister shall say to the man :

M., WILT thou have this Woman to thy wedded wife, to live together after God's ordinance, in the holy estate of matrimony ? Wilt thou love her, comfort her, honor, and keep her, in sickness and in health ; and, forsaking all others, keep thee only unto her, so long as ye both shall live ?

The man shall answer, I will.

Then shall the minister say to the woman:

N., WILT thou have this Man to thy wedded husband, to live together after God's ordinance, in the holy estate of matrimony ? Wilt thou obey him and serve him, love, honor, and keep him, in sickness and in health ; and, forsaking all others, keep thee only unto him, so long as ye both shall live ?

The woman shall answer, I will.

19

Then shall the minister say :

WHO giveth this woman to be married to this man ?

Then shall they give their Troth to each other in this manner :   The
minister, receiving the woman at her father's or friend's hands,
shall cause the man with his right hand to take the woman by
her right hand, and to say after him as follows :

I M., take thee, N., to my wedded wife, to have and to hold from this day forward, for better for worse, for richer for poorer, in sickness and in health, to love and to cherish, till death us do part, according to God's holy ordinance ; and thereto I plight thee my troth.

Then shall they loose their hands ; and the woman, with her right
hand taking the man by his right hand, shall likewise say after
the minister :

I N., take thee, M., to my wedded husband, to have and to hold from this day forward, for better for worse, for richer for poorer, in sickness and in health, to love, cherish, and to obey, till death us do part, according to God's holy ordinance ; and thereto I give thee my troth.

Then shall they again loose their hands ; and the man shall give
unto the woman a ring.   And the minister taking the ring shall
deliver it unto the man, to put it upon the fourth finger of the
woman's left hand.   And the man, holding the ring there, and
taught by the minister, shall say :

WITH this ring I thee do wed, and with all my worldly goods I thee endow : in the name of the Father, and of the Son, and of the Holy Ghost. Amen.

Then, the man leaving the ring upon the woman's left hand, the minister shall say :

Let us Pray.

OUR Father, who art in Heaven, hallowed be thy name; Thy kingdom come; Thy will be done on earth, as it is in Heaven ; Give us this day our daily bread : And forgive us our trespasses, as we forgive them that trespass against us ; And lead us not into temptation ; But deliver us from evil. Amen.

O eternal God, Creator and Preserver of all mankind, Giver of all spiritual grace, the Author of everlasting life ; send Thy blessing upon these Thy servants, this man and this woman, whom we bless in Thy name ; that, as Isaac and Rebecca lived faithfully together, so these persons may surely perform and keep the vow and covenant betwixt them made, whereof this ring given and received is a token and pledge, and may ever remain in perfect love and peace together, and live according to Thy laws; through Jesus Christ our Lord. Amen.

Then shall the minister join their right hands together, and say :

THOSE whom God hath joined together, let no man put asunder.

Then shall the minister speak unto the company :

FORASMUCH as *M.* and *N.* have consented to gether in holy wedlock, and have witnessed the same before God and this company, and thereto have given and pledged their troth, each to the other, and have declared the same by giving and receiving a ring, and by joining hands; I pronounce that they are Man and Wife, in the name of the Father, and of the Son, and of the Holy Ghost.   Amen.

And the minister shall add this blessing, the candidates kneeling, and the minister putting his hands upon their heads :

GOD the Father, God the Son, God the Holy Ghost, bless, preserve, and keep you: The Lord mercifully with His favor look upon you, and fill you with all spiritual benediction and grace ; that ye may so live together in this life, that in the world to come ye may have life everlasting.   Amen.

REGULATIONS

FOR

DELIBERATIVE ASSEMBLIES,

EMBRACING

RULES OF PARLIAMENTARY DEBATE

NOW

ACCEPTED AS AUTHORITATIVE,

AND

IN GENERAL USE.

REGULATIONS

FOR

DELIBERATIVE ASSEMBLIES

1. Bodies which hold stated meetings, such as churches, boards, religious, literary, or scientific associations, and the like, proceed directly to business on assembling, by the chairman calling the meeting to order at the appointed time. The body is supposed to be then fully organized, and the usual course is taken.

2. In religious and ecclesiastical bodies which meet annually, the officers of the previous year serve until new ones are elected. The moderator calls the meeting to order, at the time designated, and the election of officers is usually the first business, unless other service be provided for, to precede.

3. When new bodies meet, such as councils, mass-meetings, conventions called for special purposes, or persons for the formation of associations, churches, or societies, any one may call the meeting to order, when the time named arrives. If there be a committee having the matter in charge, the chairman of such committee would properly do it.

The one so calling to order names some one to take the chair, or asks the meeting to nominate some one, and puts the nomination to vote. The chairman so elected takes his seat, and completes the organization by calling for the nomination of a clerk, and other officers, if necessary. When this is done, the chairman states the object of the meeting, indicates the course of business, **and the** deliberations proceed. But if the business be difficult to reach, a committee may at once be appointed to prepare and present it in proper shape, for action before the body.

4. In some cases, where the body is large, and the business to be considered specially important or difficult, there is first a *temporary organization*, effected as above, and afterwards a *permanent organization*.

This is done by organizing temporarily with a chairman and secretary, and then proceeding to ballot for permanent officers; or by appointing a committee on nomination, which committee shall recommend persons as permanent officers. The election is usually by ballot, especially in the case of the presiding officer.

5. In representative assemblies, composed of delegates from other bodies, immediately after the first organization, the moderator calls for the credentials of delegates present, of which the clerk makes an accurate list, so as to know who has the right to a seat, and a vote in the meeting.

Neither the moderator nor the assembly can add to the number of members appointed by the bodies from which they come. Nor can any delegates regularly appointed and accredited, be deprived of their right to a seat in, and the privileges of the assembly, except for improper conduct during the meeting.

THE CHAIRMAN.

It is the duty of the presiding officer to maintain order in the assembly, and so to direct the course of proceedings as best to secure the object contemplated. He states all motions made, puts them to vote, and announces the result. He decides points of order, and appoints committees, when so directed by the body.

'f necessary for him to leave the chair, the vice-president, if there be one, takes his place; if not, and his absence be only temporary, he asks some member to occupy the chair till his return. If his absence is to be protracted, he requests the body to choose a chairman in his place

Since much of the good order and efficiency of any deliberative body depend upon the fitness of the chairman for the place, no one should be chosen for that position out of mere personal esteem, nor unless he possesses the requisite qualifications. Nor should the position be accepted by one who is conscious that he is not competent properly to discharge its duties.

In church meetings the pastor is moderator *ex officio*. But he can request any member to take the chair, if he so desires. His official position, however, would not make him chairman of a " society" meeting, where a society for secular and legal purposes is connected with the church; because the society is a distinct and separate organization from the church, though associated with it.

THE SECRETARY.

The duty of the secretary, or clerk, is, to make and keep a fair and accurate record of the proceedings of the meeting; have charge of all papers and documents belonging to it; read whatever is required to be read from the desk, before the body; call the roll of members; and furnish, when required, any information which the records contain.

1. In legislative bodies, a record of business actually passed and done constitutes the minutes. But in deliberative bodies not legislative, the records are expected to show a concise journal of all proceedings.

2. Propositions not carried, and motions lost, are not to be recorded, unless their record be ordered at the time.

3. Resolutions voted and proceedings actually had

may be omitted from the records, by a vote of the **body** at the time, so directing.

4. Names and proceedings cannot be inserted in the minutes subsequent to their approval, unless it be apparent that the omission was a mistake, and the insertion be essential to make the minutes correct.

THE MEMBERS.

All the members have equal rights and privileges in the assembly; have an equal interest in the successful issue of the deliberations; and an equal responsibility in maintaining order and furthering the business.

Discourteous remarks should not be indulged in or allowed. Members should rise to speak, and show that respect to the chairman which both his person and his position claim, and should receive.

Strict attention should be given to the proceedings. Conversation among members and all unnecessary noise should be avoided. Remarks while speaking should be confined to the subject under debate, and should be both temperate and courteous.

ORDER OF BUSINESS.

1. If the meeting be a stated one, the order of business is usually this: *First*, Reading and approval of the minutes of the last meeting. *Second*, Unfinished business, or that which appears on the minutes, including the reports of committees in their order. *Third*, New business, which may be proposed by any member.

2. If the meeting be a special one, the object and order of business may be set forth in the call by which it is convened; in which case the moderator states it, and the deliberations proceed according to that order. Or the moderator may state the object of the meeting informally, from

his own knowledge; or a committee may be appointed to prepare an order of business. Boards usually have their order of business prescribed, which order should be followed.

3. Associations and other bodies which meet annually, or at long intervals, councils and other bodies which dissolve or adjourn *sine die*, have their minutes read and corrected before adjournment.

4. The only change which can be made in the minutes, is to correct what is incorrect. If what is actually passed and done be accurately recorded, it cannot be changed to meet the wishes either of individuals or of the entire body. Entries of actual transactions cannot be obliterated. But statements of related facts, not essential to a truthful record of actual business, may be omitted in correcting the minutes, if so ordered by the body.

5. It is however expected that the minutes of churches, and other bodies not legislative, will show a concise history of their proceedings, and not be simply confined to a record of business done. This is made at the discretion of the clerk, or secretary, but is subject to revision by the body, when the minutes are passed upon.

A QUORUM.

1. In all deliberative assemblies, it is understood that the votes of a majority of members present shall decide a question, under debate.

2. In constitutional changes, and some other important matters, it is common to require a vote of two-thirds or three-fourths of those voting.

3. Boards, standing committees, and some other bodies, usually agree that no business shall be done unless there be present a certain number designated, and called a *quorum.*

4. While a majority vote strictly carries any question

ot ordinary character, yet in churches and religious assemblies, all important decisions should have the general concurrence of the body, and not be held by a mere majority.

5. Churches seldom fix the number of a *quorum* by rule, but consider any number present at a business meeting regularly called competent to act. It is however unwise to transact important business with only a small part of the church present.

MOTIONS.

1. All business must be presented by a *motion*—made in writing, if so required. Properly the motion should be made by one member and seconded by another. But routine business may by general consent pass to a vote without a second.

2. No discussion can properly be had until a motion is made, seconded, and distinctly stated by the chairman.

3. A resolution cannot be withdrawn after it has been discussed, except by unanimous consent of the body.

4. A resolution, having been discussed, must be put to vote, unless withdrawn, laid on the table, referred, or postponed.

5. A motion lost should not be recorded, unless so ordered by the body at the time.

6. A motion lost cannot be renewed at the same meeting, except by unanimous consent of the body.

7. A resolution should contain but one distinct proposition or question. If it does contain more, it must at the request of any member be divided, and the questions acted on separately.

8. Only one question can properly be before an assembly at the same time. But there are certain subsidiary motions, which by common usage may interrupt one already under debate. These are motions to *amend, to substi-*

tute, to *commit*, to *postpone*, to *lay on the table*, for *the previous question*, and to *adjourn*. These motions in their form are not debatable, except those to *amend*, and to *substitute*

9. The subsidiary motions just named cannot be interrupted by any other motion; nor can any other be applied to them, except that to *amend*, which may be done by specifying some *time*, *place*, or *purpose*.

10. Nor can these motions interrupt or supersede each other; except that a motion to adjourn is always in order, except while a speaker has the floor, or a vote is being taken.

11. When these motions, which are not debatable by usage, are amended by an addition of *time*, *place*, or *purpose*, they become debatable like other motions; but debatable only as to the time, place, or purpose, which brings them within the range of discussion.

12. No resolution or motion can be entertained, which has, at the same session been put to vote and *lost*. Nor can a resolution be entertained which directly contradicts, annuls, or abrogates one already passed. But one passed can be reconsidered and voted down, and then one of contrary import can be passed.

AMENDMENTS.

1. Amendments can be made to resolutions or motions, in three ways: by *omitting*, by *adding*, or by *substituting*, words or sentences.

2. An amendment to an amendment can be made; but not to the second degree. It would complicate and obstruct proceedings.

3. No amendment should be made which essentially changes the meaning or design of the original resolution.

4. But a *substitute* may be offered, which may or may not change the meaning of the resolution under debate.

5. An amendment is first to be discussed and acted on, and then the original resolution as amended.

SPEAKING.

1. Any member desiring to speak on a question, should rise in his place and address the moderator, confine his remarks to the question under discussion, and avoid all unkind and disrespectful language.

2. A speaker using improper language, introducing improper subjects, or otherwise out of order, should be *called to order* by the chairman, or by any member, and must either take his seat or conform to the regulations of the body.

3. A member while speaking can allow others to ask questions, or make explanations; but if he yield the floor to another, cannot claim it again as his right.

4. If two members rise at the same time to speak, preference is usually given to the one farthest from the chair, or to the one opposing the question under discussion.

5. The fact that a member has several times risen to speak, gives him no preference to be heard on that account. Nor can the moderator give the floor to one because he has made several attempts to obtain it.

6. Calls for the question cannot deprive a member of his right to speak, either when he has the floor or when rising to speak. Nor is it courteous to call for the question while a member is on the floor.

7. Should a member use offensive language in debate, his words should be taken by the clerk, verified by his own acknowledgment, or by a vote of the body, and he be required to apologize, or be visited by such censure as the body may seefit to inflict.

VOTING.

1. The question is put to vote by the chairman, having first distinctly restated it, that all may clearly understand how and on what they vote. First, the *affirmative*, then the *negative* is called ; each so deliberately as to give all an opportunity of voting. He then distinctly announces whether the motion is *carried* or *lost*.

2. Voting is done usually by *aye* and *no*, or by *raising the hand*. When the decision is doubted, by *standing to be counted*. Sometimes by *ballot*, sometimes by a *division of the house*, the affirmative taking one side and the negative the other, until counted. Sometimes by calling the *yeas* and *nays*, the clerk calling the roll, and each member answering with his vote. The last two methods are in use chiefly in legislative assemblies.

3. Taking the *yeas* and *nays* is resorted to usually for the purpose of holding members accountable to the constituents whom they represent. In churches and other voluntary associations it cannot be required, since they are not representative bodies, and have no constituencies to whom they are amenable.

4. If the *yeas* and *nays* be ordered, each member has the right to explain his vote at length ; and in doing so, can discuss the merits of the entire question, should he choose, in order to justify his vote.

5. If the vote as announced by the moderator be doubted, it is usual to call it the second time, generally by counting.

6. All members should vote, unless for reasons excused ; or those under discipline, during which disability they should take no active part in the business of the body.

7. The moderator usually votes when the question is taken by ballot; otherwise it is customary for him to waive that right. But when the assembly is equally divided, he may, if so disposed, give the casting vote.

8. When the vote is taken by ballot, as is usual on important questions, especially in the election of officers

tellers are appointed by the chair to distribute, collect, and count the ballots.

9. The tellers do not themselves announce the result of the ballot, but report it to the chairman, who makes the announcement.

10. In announcing the result, it is usual to state the whole number of votes cast, the number necessary to a choice (in the case of an election), and the number cast for the successful candidate, and then to declare his election. If there be no election, the number of votes for several of the highest candidates is announced, and a new ballot is ordered.

COMMITTEES.

1. Committees are nominated by the chairman, at the direction of the body, and their nomination confirmed by a vote. More commonly, the meeting directs that all committees shall be *appointed* by the chair; in which case no vote is needed to confirm.

2. Any matter of business, or subject under debate, may be *referred* to a committee, with or without *instructions.* The committee make their *report,* which is the result of their deliberations. The body then takes action on the report, and on any *recommendations* it may contain.

3. The report of a committee is *received* by a vote, which acknowledges their service, and takes their report before the body for consideration. Afterwards, any distinct *recommendation* contained in the report is acted on, and may be adopted or rejected.

4. Frequently, however, when the recommendations of the committee are of trifling moment, or likely to be generally acceptable, the report is *received* and *adopted* by a single vote.

5. A report may be *recommitted* to the committee, or

that committee may be discharged, and another **appointed** for the same purpose, with or without instructions, for a further consideration of the subject, so as to present it in a form more likely to secure the concurrence of the body.

6. The meeting has no power to change the form of a committee's report; for then, so far, it would be a document of the body, and not of the committee. But the report may be recommitted with instructions to change it. Any distinct recommendation in the report may, however, be modified, since that, if adopted, becomes the action of the body, rather than of the committee.

7. A committee may be appointed *with power* for a specific purpose. In that case it has full discretion to dispose conclusively of the business intrusted to it, without further reference to the body.

8. The first one named in the appointment of a committee, is by courtesy considered the *chairman*. But a committee, when called together, has the right to elect its own chairman.

9. The member who moves the appointment of a committee, is usually out of courtesy, though not necessarily, appointed, first named on it, and acts as chairman.

10. Committees of arrangement, or for other business protracted in its nature, *report progress* from time to time, and are *continued* until their final report is made, or their appointment expires by limitation.

11. A committee is *discharged* by a vote when its business is done, and its reports received. But usually a committee is considered as discharged by the acceptance of its report.

12. In constituting a committee, it is usual to appoint a majority of those *favorable* to the proposition submitted to their consideration, if it be a matter in controversy.

13. In making up its report, if unanimity cannot be

20*

secured, a majority prepares and presents the report. But the *minority* may also present a separate report. The body can hear and act on both, at its discretion; or it may refuse to give any consideration to the minority report, if so disposed.

STANDING COMMITTEES.

A committee appointed to act for a given time, or during the recess of the body is called a *standing committee*. It has charge of a given department of business assigned oy the body; acts either with power in the final disposition of that business, or under instructions, in preparing it for the action of the body. A standing committee is substantially a minor board, and has it own chairman, secretary, records, times of meeting, and order of business.

COMMITTEE OF THE WHOLE.

When an assembly desires to consider any subject in a manner less formal and restricted than can be done under ordinary rules of business, it may resolve itself into a *committee of the whole* for that purpose.

This is done by a vote to *go into a committee of the whole,* at a given time, and for a given purpose. When the specified time arrives, the presiding officer names some member to take the chair, the business is stated, and the body, as committee, proceeds to its consideration.

The proceedings are governed by the ordinary rules of debate, except—

1. The chairman has the same privileges in debate as other members.

2. Speakers are not restricted as to time.

3. The previous question cannot be called.

4. No committees can be appointed.

5. No other business than that assigned can be considered by them.

6. The committee cannot *adjourn*, but *rise,* when its
time has expired; and if its business be not completed,
it will, when its report is made, ask permission of the assembly to sit again.

When the committee *rises*, the moderator of the body
resumes his seat, and the chairman of the committee reports the results of the deliberations. This form of committee is seldom resorted to except in legislative bodies.

APPEAL.

The moderator announces all votes, and decides all
questions as to rules of proceeding, and order in debate.
But any member who is dissatisfied with his decisions
may *appeal* from it, to the decision of the body.   The
moderator then puts the question, " *Shall the decision of
the chair be sustained ?* "   The vote on this question is
final. The question on appeal is not debatable. The
right of appeal is undeniable, but should not be too freely
used.

PROTEST.

It is the right of any member, who may regard the action of the body in a given case, to be wrong, unauthor-
ized, or in any way oppressive, to *protest* against it.   This
protest may be made verbally and informally ; in which
case it is heard, but is not entered on the minutes except
by request of the protestant, and by permission of the
body.   But if it be presented formally in writing, the
body is bound to receive the document, and record its reception.   The entire document can be entered on the records by a vote of the body.

The right of *protest*, as well as that of *petition* and *appeal*, can never be denied to free men without an abridg-

ment of their liberties. Questions pertaining to the rights and privileges of members, even though they be liable to abuse, should be treated by deliberative assemblies, in the most liberal manner, consistent with good order and a proper discharge of their obligations.

THE PREVIOUS QUESTION.

Debate may be cut short by a vote to take the *previous question.* By this is meant that the previous, original or main question under discussion, be immediately voted on, regardless of pending amendments and secondary questions, and without further debate.

In some bodies, a motion for the previous question cannot be entertained, unless such motion be *seconded* by one quarter, one third, or one half—as the rule may be—of the voters present. But in bodies where no rule exists, a motion made and seconded like any other, is sufficient if it be voted by a majority. A motion for the previous question is not debatable.

1 If a motion for the previous question be *carried,* then the main question must be immediately taken, without further debate.

2. If the motion for the previous question be *lost,* the debate proceeds as though no such motion had been made.

3. The previous question cannot be ordered while a motion to *postpone,* or to *commit,* is under consideration. It cannot itself be *postponed,* nor *amended ;* but it can be interrupted by a motion to *lay on the table* the original resolution, which if voted, carries with it the whole subject under debate, including the motion for the previous question.

4. If a motion for the previous question be *lost,* it cannot be renewed on the same question during that session, unless the question has undergone some change by amendment, or otherwise, in the mean time.

LAY ON THE TABLE.

Immediate and decisive action on any question under debate, may be deferred, by a vote to *lay on the table* the resolution pending. This disposes of the whole question for the present, and ordinarily, is in effect a final dismissal of it. But any member has the right subsequently to call it up by a motion. The body decides by vote, whether it will, or will not take it up. A motion to lay on the table is not debatable.

1. Sometimes, however, a resolution is laid on the table for the present, or until a specified time, to give place for other business necessary to be done. It is then called up, when the time specified arrives.

2. A motion to lay on the table, must apply to a resolution or other documentary matters. There must be something to lay on the table. An abstract subject cannot be disposed of in this way.

POSTPONEMENT.

A simple *postponement* is for a specified time or purpose, the business to be resumed when this time or purpose is reached. But a question *indefinitely postponed,* is considered as fully dismissed.

NOT DEBATABLE.

Certain motions, by established usage, are *not debatable,* but when once before the body, must be put to vote without discussion.

These are : the *previous question ;* for *indefinite postponement ;* to *commit ;* to *lay on the table ;* on *appeal ;* to *adjourn.* But when these motions are modified by some condition of *time, place,* or *purpose,* they become debatable, and subject to the rules of other motions; but are

debatable so far only as concerns the time, place, or pur·
pose by which they are modified.

A body is however competent, by a vote, to allow debate on all motions.

TO RECONSIDER.

1. A motion to *reconsider* a motion already passed,
according to established usage, must be made by one who
voted *for* that motion when it passed.

2. If the body decides to *reconsider*, then the motion or
resolution so reconsidered, is placed before them, as it was
previous to its passage, and may be discussed, adopted, or
rejected.

3. A vote to reconsider, should be taken at the same
session, at which the vote reconsidered was passed ; and
also, when there are as many members present as voted
on it then.

BE DISCUSSED.

If when a motion is introduced, a member objects to its
discussion as foreign, profitless, or contentious, the moderator should at once put the question, " *Shall this motion
be discussed ?* " If it be decided in the negative, the mo
tion cannot be entertained.

ORDER OF THE DAY.

The body may decide to take up some particular business at a specified time. That business thereby becomes
the *order of the day*, for the time specified. When the
hour arrives, it must be taken up by the call of the chair·
man, or of any member, with or without a vote, all pending
business being postponed in consequence.

POINT OF ORDER.

Any member who supposes a speaker to be out of order, or that a discussion is proceeding improperly, may at any time *rise to a point of order.* He must distinctly state his question or objection, and the chairman must decide whether his objection be well taken.

But one rising to a point of order cannot discuss the question, nor enter into any debate; he must simply state his objection, and wait for a decision.

PRIVILEGED QUESTIONS.

Questions relating to the *rights* and *privileges* of members are of primary importance, and until disposed of take precedence of all other business, and supersede all other questions, except that of adjournment.

RULE SUSPENDED.

A rule of order may be *suspended* by a vote of the body to allow the transaction of business, which could not otherwise be done without a violation of such rule. But if rules be thought necessary to exist, they should not frequently be suspended.

FILLING BLANKS.

Where different numbers are suggested for filling blanks, the *highest number, greatest distance,* and *longest time* are usually voted on first.

ADJOURNMENT.

1. A simple motion *to adjourn* is always in order, except while one is speaking, or a vote is being taken. It takes precedence of all other questions, and is not debatable.

2. In some deliberative bodies a motion to adjourn is in order while speaking or voting is going on, the business to stand on re-assembling precisely as it was when adjournment took place.

3. A body may adjourn to a specified time. But if no time be mentioned, the fixed or usual time is understood. If there be no fixed or usual time, then an adjournment without date is equivalent to a dissolution.

4. A body may, at any stage of its proceedings, vote that it will adjourn at a given time. When that time arrives, the chairman will call for a vote of adjournment, or declare the meeting adjourned without further action.

5. A body may, at any stage of its proceedings, vote that when it does adjourn, it will adjourn to a given time. That vote will therefore fix the time of its re-assembling, without any further action.

ECCLESIASTICAL

Forms and Blanks,

INCLUDING

1 ETTERS, MINUTES, CERTIFICATES, COUN
CILS, CONVENTIONS,

AND

LICENSES.

FORMS AND BLANKS.

.

ECCLESIASTICAL FORMS and Blanks have no
fixed or necessary wording. They will vary
according to the customs of the churches, and the
taste of those who prepare them. The following
present substantially the forms in common use:

---

1. LETTER OF DISMISSION.

The ——— Church of ———
   To the ——— Church of ———,
   Dear Brethren:
   This is to certify, that ——— is a member of this
church in good and regular standing, and, at ———
own · request, is hereby dismissed from us, for the
purpose of uniting with you. When ——— shall
have so united, ——— connection with us will cease.
May the blessing of God rest on ——— and you.
   Done by order of the Church.
   New York, Nov. —, 18—.
                     ——— ———, Clerk.
   This Letter is valid for six months from date.

NOTE 1.—Letters are usually limited as to their va-
lidity; more commonly to six months. This is to se-

cure their speedy use. If not used within that time, they can be renewed, at the discretion of the church.

NOTE 2.—It is customary to ask for a letter to some specified church, which is named in the letter given. But it may be given to " any church of the same faith and order," when the member is uncertain as to what church it may be presented. Or if given for one church, it is equally valid if presented to another.

NOTE 3.—It is desirable that some church should be specified in the letter given ; but this is not necessary, and a church has no right to refuse to give a letter because the member asking it does not specify some particular church.

NOTE 4.—When letters are granted, and members dismissed for the purpose of constituting a new church, that fact should be stated in the letters.

NOTE 5.—Members receiving letters do not cease their connection with the church, but continue under its watch and discipline, until they have actually united with another church.

2. LETTER OF COMMENDATION.

NEW YORK, Nov. —, 18—,

This certifies that ——— ——— is a member in good standing, in the ——— ——— church, in ——— and is hereby commended to the confidence, sympathy and fellowship of sister churches, wherever Providence may direct ——— course.

——— ———,

Pastor ——— Church.

NOTE.—This form of letter, sometimes called a letter of " Occasional Communion," is for members during a temporary absence from home. It may be given by the pastor, or by the clerk, as authorized by the church. It should be returned to the pastor, or clerk, on the return of the member.

---

3. LETTER OF NOTIFICATION.

NEW YORK, Nov. —, 18—.

To the ——— Church.

Dear Brethren :

This certifies that ——— ——— was received by letter from you, to membership in the ——— Church, Nov. — 18—.

——— ———, Ch. Clerk.

NOTE 1.—This form is by many churches sent with every letter of dismission granted, and is to be filed by the clerk of the church receiving said member, and returned to the church which granted the letter, as a notification of reception.

NOTE 2.—The church granting letters does not drop the members dismissed until they have information of their having actually united elsewhere.

---

4. MINUTES OF CHURCH MEETING.

NEW YORK, Nov. —, 18—.

The Church held its regular meeting for business, this evening, at — o'clock.

The pastor was Moderator.

21*

After singing, and reading the Scriptures, **prayer** was offered by ———.

The minutes of the last meeting were read and approved.

[Then follows a clear and faithful record of all business transacted.]

The meeting adjourned.

——— ———, Clerk.

NOTE 1.—The records of a church should show, not only the bare minutes of the business actually done, but a concise history of its progress, embracing all the important changes, incidents and events which constitute its material history.

NOTE 2.—All business should be taken up and transacted in an orderly manner. It is to be pursued under two general divisions.

1. Unfinished business : that which has come over from a previous meeting, and is presented by the minutes; embracing the reports of committees, and other items, in their order.

2. New business: such as may come up at the time, presented by the pastor, deacons, or other members.

---

5. CALL FOR AN ORDAINING COUNCIL.

NEW YORK, Nov. —, 18—

The ——— Church of ———

To the ——— Church of ———.

Dear Brethren:

You are requested to send your pastor and two

brethren, to sit in council with us, Dec. —, at --
o'clock P. M., to consider the propriety of setting
apart to the work of the gospel ministry, our
brother ——— ———.

The Council will meet in ———.

The following churches are invited ———.

By order of the Church,

——— ———, Clerk.

NOTE 1.—The letters, by which the council is called, should be issued by the Church, and not by the
candidate.

NOTE 2.—The candidate should be a member of
the Church calling the council, as it would not be
proper for a Church to call a council for the examination and ordination of one to whom they sustained no
ecclesiastical relation.

NOTE 3.—Consequently, if a candidate accepts the
call of a church to become its pastor, he should unite
with that church before it calls a council for his
ordination.

NOTE 4.—But if, for any reason, it should be
thought desirable for the candidate to be ordained in
the Church of which he was a member, and before
his membership shall be transferred, it would be
proper for the Church which had called him, to lay
before his Church the facts, and request them to call
a council for that purpose, in order that he might
become their pastor.

NOTE 5.—It is not desirable that a man should
receive ordination until some definite sphere of ministerial labor is open to him. One of the evidences of
his divine call lies in the fact that his gifts are acceptable, and his services are demanded in some department of ministerial work.

6. CALL FOR A RECOGNIZING COUNCIL.

NEW YORK, Nov.—, 18—.

To the ——— Church in ———.

Dear Brethren:

In behalf of a company of believers in Christ, you are requested to send your pastor and two brethren, to meet in council at ———, Dec. —, at — o'clock P. M., to consider the propriety of recognizing said company of believers, as a regular and independent Church.

The Council will meet in ———.

The following churches are invited ———.

Affectionately yours,

——— ———, Com. or Clerk.

7. CALL FOR AN ADVISORY COUNCIL.

NEW YORK, Nov.—, 18—.

The ——— Church of ———

To the ——— Church of ———.

Dear Brethren :

You are requested to send your pastor and two brethren, to sit in council Dec. —, at — o'clock P. M., to advise concerning certain difficulties existing among us, which disturb our peace, and threaten serious consequences to the welfare of the Church.

The Council will be held in ———.

The following churches are invited ———.

By order of the Church,

——— ———, Clerk.

NOTE 1.—The letters by which a council is convened are called *letters missive*, and constitute the warrant for the meeting of the body, and the charter under which it acts. These letters should if possible state distinctly and specifically the matters to be presented to the body when convened.

NOTE 2.—By common usage and general agreement, a council cannot take action on or investigate any subject, not embraced in the call by which it is convened.

NOTE 3.—A council may be called to give advice, not only in respect to difficulties, but with regard to any matter on which the Church may wish to be advised.

NOTE 4.—A council may be called either by a *church* or by *individuals*. A *mutual* council is one called by the mutual action and agreement of the different parties to a difficulty. An *ex parte* council is one called by one of the parties to a difficulty.

NOTE 5.—An *ex parte* council should not be called to adjust a difficulty, until all reasonable efforts have failed to secure a *mutual* council to which that difficulty may be referred.

8. MINUTES OF A COUNCIL.

NEW YORK, Nov. —, 18—.

An Ecclesiastical Council, called by the ——— church, convened in ——— this day, at — o'clock P. M.

Organized by choosing ——— ——— Moderator, and ——— ——— Clerk

Prayer was offered by ———— ————.

The letter by which the Council was called, and the records of the church in reference thereto, were read, stating the object to be . . . . . .

The credentials of messengers were presented.

The following brethren were present from the following churches :—

Brethren.	Churches.
————	—— ——
————	—— ——
————	—— ——

[Then follows a faithful record of the proceedings.]

The Council dissolved, after prayer by ———— ————.

———— ————, Moderator.
———— ————, Clerk.

NOTE 1.—A true and faithful record of the proceedings of the body should be made by the Clerk, read, and approved by the body before adjournment, and signed by the Moderator and Clerk.

NOTE 2.—A copy of the minutes, duly certified and signed by the officers, should be furnished to the parties calling the Council.

———————

9. MINUTES OF A COMMITTEE.

NEW YORK, Nov. —, 18—.

The ———— Committee met, at ————, at ———— o'clock P. M.

Present ———— ———— ———— ———— ————.

Brother ———— ———— in the chair.

Prayer by ———— ————.

The minutes of the last meeting were read and approved.

[Then follows a record of business.]

Adjourned.

——— ———, Secretary.

———————————

10. MINUTES OF A CONVENTION.

NEW YORK, Nov. ——, 18——.

A Convention called to consider ——— ——— ——— ——— ——— ——— met in ———, at ———, at ——— o'clock P. M.

——— ——— was chosen Chairman, and ——— ——— Secretary.

After prayer by ——— ———, the Chairman stated the object of the meeting to be ——— ——— ——— ——— ———.

[Then follows a record of proceedings.]

The Convention then adjourned.

——— ———, Chairman.

——— ———, Secretary.

NOTE.—The rules for all meetings of deliberative bodies, whether churches, councils, conventions, or committees, are substantially the same. But every body has the right to form rules for itself, and regulate its own order of business. If a meeting adopts no rules, then it must be governed by the usual parlimentary order.

———————————

11. FORM OF LICENSE.

It is customary for churches to give a *license to*

those who are believed to have been divinely called
to preach the gospel, but are not yet prepared to be
ordained and enter fully upon the work of the ministry. A license, however, is not necessary, nor does
it give any authority, or impart any qualification. It
is simply a certificate of approval and commendation, by the church giving it.

The following form may be varied according to
pleasure or circumstances:

LICENSE.

This certifies that Brother ——— ——— is a member of the ——— ——— church, in good and regular
standing, and is held by us in high esteem. We believe him to have been called of God to the work of
the gospel ministry, and do hereby give him our entire and cordial approbation in the improvement of his
gifts, by preaching the gospel, as Providence may
afford him opportunity. And we pray the great
Head of the Church to endow him with all needful
grace, and crown his labors with abundant success.

Done by order of the church, this day, Nov. —,
18—.   ——— ———, Pastor.

——— ———, Clerk.

NOTE.—Licentiates are not recognized by law, as
regularly ordained clergymen, and are not therefore
competent to solemnize marriages. Nor is it cus
tomary for them to administer the ordinances. But
it is entirely proper for a church, in the absence of
an ordained minister, to authorize a licentiate, or
even a layman, to administer the ordinances for
them. For them, though not for others.

12. CERTIFICATE OF ORDINATION.

This certifies that our Brother ——— ——— was publicly set apart to the work of the gospel ministry, with prayer and the laying on of hands, by the authority of the ——— ——— church, and according to the usages of our denomination, at ——— ———, Nov. —, 18—.

That he was called to ordination by the ——— church, of which he was a member, and which, after full and sufficient opportunity to judge, were agreed in the opinion that he was called of God to the work of the ministry.

That ——— churches were represented in the council, by ——— ministers, and ——— laymen; and that after a full, fair and deliberate examination, being satisfied on all points, the council did unanimously recommend his ordination.

That our Brother ——— ——— did accordingly receive the full, entire and hearty approval of the council in his officially entering upon the work of the ministry, preaching the Word, administering the ordinances, and performing all those duties, and enjoying all those privileges, to which a minister of Christ is called, and entitled.

And may the blessing of the great Head of the Church attend him, crown his labors with abundant success, and make him an honored instrument of good to Zion, and the World.

——— ———, Moderator.
——— ———, Clerk.

New York, Nov. —, 18—
22

BIBLE PROPER NAMES,

WITH THEIR

Pronunciation and Signification,

AS USED IN

THE SCRIPTURES.

TABLE

OF

SCRIPTURE PROPER NAMES.

AB	AD
A 'A-RON, a teacher, or lofty.	Ab'i-tai, the father of the dew.
A-bad'don, the destroyer.	Ab'i-tub, father of goodness.
A-bag'tha, father of the wine-press.	Ab'i-ud, father of praise.
Ab'a-na, made of stone, a building.	Ab'ner, father of light.
Ab'a-rim, passages, or passengers.	A'bram, a high father.
Ab'da, a servant, or servitude.	A'bra-ham, the father of a great multitude.
Ab'di, he is my servant.	Ab'sa-lom, father of peace.
Ab'di-el, the servant of God.	Ac'cad, a vessel, a pitcher, or sparkle.
Ab'don, servant, or cloud of judgment.	Ac'cho, close pressed together.
A-bed'ne-go, a servant of light.	A-cel'da-ma, the field of blood.
A'bel, vanity, breath, vapor.	A-cha'i-a, grief or trouble.
A'bel, (a city,) mourning.	A-cha'i-cus, a native of Achaia.
A'bel-beth-ma-ach'ah, mourning to the house of Maachah.	A'chan, or Ach'ar, he that troubleth.
A'bel-ma'im, mourning of waters.	Aeh'bor, a rat.
A'bel-me-ho'lah, mourning of sickness.	A'chim, preparing, or revenging.
A'bel-miz-ra'im, the mourning of the Egyptians.	A'chish, thus it is, or how is this?
	Ach-me'tha, a city.
A'bel-shit'tim, mourning of thorns	A'chor, trouble.
A'bez, an egg, or muddy.	Ach'sah, adorned, bursting the veil.
A'bi, my father.	Ach'shaph, poison, tricks.
A-bi'ah, the Lord is my father.	Ach'zib, liar, lying, or that runs.
A-bi-al'bon, most intelligent father.	Ad'a-dah, the witness of the assembly.
A-bi'a-thar, excellent father.	A'dah, an assembly.
A'bib, green fruits, or ears of corn.	A-dai'ah, the witness of the Lord.
A-bi'dah, the father of knowledge.	A-da-li'ah, one that draws water.
A-bi'dan, the father of judgment.	Ad'am, earthy man, red.
Ab'i-el, God my father.	Ad'a-mah, red earth, or of blood.
A-bi-e'zer, father of help.	Ad'a-mi, my man, red, earthy, human.
Ab'i-gail, the father's joy.	A'dar, high or eminent.
Ab-i-ha'il, the father of strength.	Ad'be-el, a vapor, a cloud of God.
A-bi'hu, he is my father.	Ad'di, my witness, adorned, prey.
A-bi'jah, the Lord is my father.	Ad'don, basis, foundation, the Lord.
A-bi'jam, father of the sea.	A'di-el, the witness of the Lord.
Ab-i-le'ne, the father of mourning.	A'din, adorned, voluptuous, dainty.
A-bim'a-el, a father sent from God.	A-di-tha'im, assemblies, testimonies.
A-bim'e-lech, father of the king.	Ad'la-i, my witness, my ornament.
A-bin'a-dab, father of willingness.	Ad'mah, earthy, red, or bloody.
A-bin'o-am, father of beauty.	Ad'ma-tha, a cloud of death, a mortal vapor.
A-bi'ram, a high father.	Ad'nah, rest, or testimony eternal.
Ab'i-shag, ignorance of the father.	A-do-ni-be'zek, the lightning of the Lord, or the Lord of lightning.
A-bish'a-i, the present of my father.	A-do-ni'jah, the Lord is my master.
A-bish'a-lom, the father of peace.	A-don'i-kam, the Lord is raised.
A-bish'u-a, father of salvation.	A-do-ni'ram, my Lord is most high, or Lord of might and elevation.
Ab'i-shur, the father of the wall, or father of uprightness.	A-do-ni-ze'dek, justice of the Lord.

AD	AS
A-do'ram, their beauty, their power.	A'mos, loading, weighty.
A-do-ra'im, strength of the sea.	A'moz, strong, robust.
A-dram'me-lech, the cloak, glory, grandeur, or power of the king.	Am-phil'o-lis, a city encompassed by the sea.
A-dram-yt'ti-um, the court of death.	Am'pli-as, large, extensive.
A'dri-a, a city, which gives name to the Adriatic sea, now the gulf of Venice.	Am'ram, an exalted people, their sheaves or handfuls of corn.
A-dul'lam, their testimony, their prey, or their ornament.	Am'ra-phel, one that speaks of secrets.
	A'nah, one who answers, or afflicted.
Ag'a-bus, a locust, feast of the father.	A'nak, a collar, or ornament.
A'gag, roof, floor.	A-nam'me-lech, answer, song of the king and council.
A'gar. See Hagar.	
A-grip'pa, one who causes great pain at his birth.	An-a-ni'as, the cloud of the Lord.
	An'a-thoth, answer, song, or poverty.
A'gur, stranger, gathered together.	An'drew, a stout and strong man.
A'hab, uncle, or father's brother.	An-dron'i-cus, a man excelling others.
A-has-ue'rus, prince, head, or chief.	A'ner, answer, song, affliction.
A-ba'va, essence or generation.	An'na, gracious, or one who gives.
A'haz, one that takes and possesses.	An'nas, one who answers, humble.
A-ne-ziah, seizure, vision of the Lord.	An'ti-christ, an adversary to Christ.
A-hi'ah, brother of the Lord.	An'ti-och, speedy as a chariot.
A-hi-e'zer, brother of assistance.	An'ti-pas, for all or against all.
A-hi'jah, the same with Ahiah.	An-tip'a-tris, for, or against the father.
A-hi'kam, a brother who rises up.	A-pel'les, exclusion, separation.
A-hi'lud, a brother born.	A'phek, a stream, a rapid torrent.
A-him'a-za, brother of the council.	A-po-lo'ni-a, perdition, destruction.
A-hi'man, brother of the right hand.	A-pol'los, who destroys, or wastes.
A-him'e-lech, my brother is a king.	A-pol'ly-on, one who exterminates.
A-hi'moth, brother of death.	Ap'phi-a, productive, fruitful.
A-hin'o-am, the beauty of the brother, or brother of motion.	Ap'pi-i Fo'rum, a town so called from Appius Claudius, whose statue was erected there
A-hi'o, his brother, his brethren.	Aq'ui-la, an eagle.
A-hi'ra, brother of iniquity; or brother of the shepherd.	Ar, awaking or uncovering.
	A-ra'bia, evening, wild and desert.
A-his-a-mach, brother of strength.	A'ram, highness, magnificence, or one that deceives, or their curse.
A-hi'shar, brother of a prince, or brother of a song.	Ar'a-rat, the curse of trembling.
A-hi'ho-phel, brother of ruin or folly.	Ar-au'nah, ark, song, joyful cry.
A-hi'tub, brother of goodness.	Ar'ba, city of the four.
A-hi'hud, brother of praise.	Ar-che-la'us, the prince of the people.
Ah'lab, which is of milk, or of fat.	Ar-chip'pus, the chief of the stables.
A-ho'lah, his tabernacle, his tent.	Arc-tu'rus, a gathering together.
A-ho'li-ab, the tent or tabernacle of the father.	A'rd, one that commands, or he that descends.
A-ho'li-bah, my tent and my tabernacle in her.	A-re'li, the light or vision of God.
A-ho'li-ba-mah, my tabernacle is exalted.	A-re-op'a-gus, the hill of Mars.
A'i, or Ha'i, mass or heap.	Ar'e-tas, agreeable, virtuous.
A-i'ath, the same as Ai.	Ar'gob, a turf, or fat land.
A'ja-lon, a chain, strength, or stag.	A'ri-el, altar, light or lion of God.
A-lam'me-lech, God is king.	Ar-i-ma-the'a, a lion dead to the Lord.
Al-ex-an'der, one who assists men.	A'ri-och, long, great, tall.
Al-ex-an'dri-a, a city in Egypt.	Ar-is-tar'chus, a good prince, or the best prince.
Al-le-lu'ia, praise the Lord.	
Al'lon, an oak, or strong.	Ar-is-to-bu'lus, a good counsellor.
Al'lon-bach'uth, the oak of weeping.	Ar-ma-ged'don, mountain of the gospel, or of Meggido.
Al-mo'dad, measure of God.	
Al'pha, the first letter of the Greek alphabet, marked A.	Ar-me'ni-a, a province which is supposed to take its name from Aram.
Al-phe'us, a thousand, learned, or chief.	Ar'non, rejoicing, leaping for joy.
Am'a-lek, a people that licks up.	Ar'o-er, heath, tamarisk.
Am'a-na, integrity and truth.	Ar'pad, the light of redemption.
Am-a-ri'ah, the Lord says, or the excellency of the Lord.	Ar-phax'ad, a healer of desolation.
	Ar-tax-er-xes, the silence of light.
Am-a'sa, sparing the people.	Ar'te-mas, whole, sound.
Am-a-zi'ah, the strength of the Lord.	A'sa, physician, or cure.
Am'mah, my people.	As'a-hel, work or creature of God.
Am'mi, the same with Ammah.	As-a-i'ah, the Lord hath wrought.
Am-min'a-dib, my people is liberal.	A'saph, who assembles the people.
Am-mi'hud, people of praise.	As'e-nath, peril, or misfortune.
Am-mi-shad'da-i, the people of the Almighty, the Almighty is with me.	Ash'dod, effusion, inclination, theft.
	Ash'er, happiness.
Am'mon, a people, son of my people.	Ash'i-ma, crime, position.
Am'non, faithful and true, or tutor.	Ash'ke-naz, a fire that spreads.
A'mon, faithful, true.	Ash'ta-roth, flocks, sheep, or riches.
Am'o-rite, bitter, a rebel, a babbler.	Ash'ur, who is happy, walks looks.
	A'si-a, muddy, boggy.

AS

As'ke-lon, weight, balance, or fire of infamy.
As-nap'per, unhappiness, or increase of danger.
As'sir, prisoner, fettered.
As'sos, approaching, coming near.
A-syn'cri-tus, incomparable.
A'tad, a thorn.
Ath-a-li'ah, the time of the Lord.
Ath'ens, so called from Athene, or Athenaia, Minerva.
Att-a-li'a, that increases or sends.
Au-gus'tus, increased, augmented.
A'ven, iniquity, force, riches.
Az-a-ri'ah, he that hears the Lord.
A-ze'kah, strength of walls.
Az'gad, a strong army, strength of fortune, or a gang of robbers.
A2-noth'-ta'bor, the ears of Tabor, or the ears of purity or contrition.
A-zo'tus, the same as Ashdod.
A'zur, he that assists, or is assisted.

B A'AL, he that rules and subdues.
Ba'al-ah, her idol, or she that is governed or subdued, a spouse.
Ba'al-be'rith, idol of the covenant.
Ba'al-gad', idol of fortune or of felicity.
Ba'al-ha'mon, who rules a crowd.
Ba'al-her'mon, possessor of destruction, or of a thing cursed.
Ba'al-i, my idol, or lord over me.
Ba'al-im, idols, masters, false gods.
Ba'al-is, a rejoicing, or a proud lord.
Ba'al-me'on, idol or master of the house.
Ba'al-pe'or, master of the opening.
Ba'al-per-a'zim, god of divisions.
Ba'al-shal'i-sha, the god that presides over three, the third idol.
Ba'al-ta'mar, master of the palm-tree.
Ba'al-ze'bub, the god of the fly.
Ba'al-ze'phon, the idol or possession of the north, hidden, secret.
Ba'a-nah, in the answer, in affliction.
Ba'a-shah, he that seeks, or lays waste.
Ba'bel, confusion or mixture.
Ba'by-lon. See Babel.
Ba'ca, a mulberry-tree.
Ba-hu'rim, choice, warlike, valiant.
Ba'jith, a house.
Ba'laam, the ancient of the people.
Ba'lak, who lays waste or destroys.
Ba'mah, an eminence, or high place.
Ba-rab'bas, son of shame, confusion.
Bar'a-chel, that bows before God.
Bar-a-chi'as, the same with Barachel.
Ba'rak, thunder, or in vain.
Bar-je'sus, son of Jesus of Joshua.
Bar-jo'na, son of Jona, or of a dove.
Bar'na-bas, son of the prophet, or of consolation.
Bar'sa-bas, son of return, son of rest.
Bar-thol'o-mew, a son that suspends the waters.
Bar-ti-me'us, son of the honorable.
Ba'ruch, who is blessed.
Bar-zil'la-i, son of contempt.
Ba'shan, in the tooth, or in the ivory.
Bash'e-math, perfumed, confusion of death, or in desolation.
Bath'-she-ba, the seventh daughter, or the daughter of satiety.
Be'dad, alone, solitary.
Be'dan, according to judgment.
Be-el'ze-bub. See Baal-zebub.

CA

Be'er, a well.
Be'er-la-ha-i'roi, the well of him that liveth and seeth me.
Be'er-she'ba, the well of an oath.
Be'kah, half a shekel.
Bel, ancient, or nothing.
Be'li-al, wicked, of no account.
Bel-shaz'zar, master of the treasure.
Bel-te-shaz'zar, who lays up treasures in secret.
Be-na-i'ah, son of the Lord.
Ben-am'mi, son of my people.
Ben'ha-dad, son of Hadad, or of noise.
Ben'ja-min, son of the right hand.
Be-no'ni, son of my sorrow, or pain.
Be'or, burning, foolish, mad.
Ber'a-chah, blessing, bending the knee.
Be-re'a, heavy, weighty.
Be'rith, covenant.
Ber-ni'ce, one that brings victory.
Be'sor, glad news, or incarnation.
Be'tah, confidence.
Beth-ab'a-ra, the house of passage.
Beth'a-ny, the house of song, or of affliction.
Beth'a-ven, the house of vanity, of iniquity, of trouble.
Beth-bir'e-i, the house of my Creator, the house of my health.
Beth'car, the house of the lamb.
Beth-da'gon, the house of corn.
Beth-dib-la-tha'im, house of dry figs.
Beth'el, the house of God.
Be'ther, division, or in the trial.
Be-thes'da, house of pity, or mercy.
Beth-e'zal, a neighbor's house.
Beth-ga'mul, the house of recompense.
Beth-hac'ce-rem, the house of the vineyard.
Beth-ho'ron, the house of wrath.
Beth'le-hem, the house of bread.
Beth-pe'or, house of gaping, or opening.
Beth'phage, the house of the mouth.
Beth-sa'i-da, house of fruits, or of food, or of snares.
Beth'-shan, house of the tooth.
Beth'she-mesh, house of the sun.
Be-thu'el, filiation of God.
Ben'lah, married.
Be-zal'e-el, in the shadow of God.
Be'zek, lightning, or in the chains
Bich'ri, first-born, first fruits.
Bid'kar, in compunction, or sharp pain.
Bin'than, in the press.
Bil'dad, old friendship, old love.
Bil'hah, who is old or confused.
Bir'sha, in evil, or son who beholds.
Bi-thi'ah, daughter of the Lord.
Bith'ron, division.
Bi-thyn'ia, violent precipitation.
Blas'tus, that buds and brings forth.
Bo-a-ner'ges, sons of thunder.
Bo'az, or Booz, in strength.
Bo'chim, the place of weeping.
Bo'zez, mud, bog.
Boz'rah, in tribulation or distress.
Bul, old age, perishing.
Buz, despised, or plundered.
Bu'zi, my contempt.

C A'BUL, displeasing, or dirty.
Ca-i'a-phas, he that seeks with diligence one that vomiteth.
Cai'n, possession, or possessed.
Ca-i'nan, possessor, or purchaser.

CA	EL

Ca'lah, favorable, opportunity.
Ca'leb, a dog, a crow, a basket.
Ca'leb-e-phra'tah. See Ephratah.
Cal'neh, our consummation.
Cal'no, our consummation, or altogether himself.
Cal'va-ry, the place of a skull.
Ca'mon, his resurrection.
Ca'na, zeal, jealousy, or possession.
Ca'na-an, merchant, trade, or that humbles and subdues.
Can-da'ce, who possesses contrition.
Ca-per'na-um, the field of repentance, or city of comfort.
Caph'tor, a sphere, buckle, or hand.
Cap-pa-do'ci-a, the same as Caphtor.
Car'cas, the covering of a lamb.
Car'che-mish, a lamb, as taken away, withdrawn.
Car'mel, circumcised lamb, harvest, full ears of corn.
Car'mi, my vineyard, or lamb of the waters.
Car'pus, fruit, or fruitful.
Ca-siph'i-a, money, or covetousness.
Ce'dron, black, or sad.
Cen'chre-a, millet, small pulse.
Ce'phas, a rock or stone.
Ce'sar, a name applicable to those who are cut out of the womb.
Ces-a-re'a, a bush of hair.
Chal'col, who nourishes, consumes, and sustains the whole.
Chal-de'a, as demons, or as robbers.
Char'ran, a singing, or calling out.
Che'bar, force, strength, as the sun.
Ched-or-la'o-mer, roughness of a sheaf.
Chem'a-rims, the name of the priests of Baal.
Che'mosh, as handling or stroking, or taking away.
Che-na-ni'ah, preparation, or disposition, or strength of the Lord.
Cher'eth-ims, who cut or tear away.
Cher'eth-ites. See Cherethims.
Che'rith, cutting, piercing, slaying.
Che'sed, as a devil, or a destroyer.
Chil'a-ab, totality, or the perfection of the father.
Chil-li'on, finished, complete, perfect.
Chil'mad, as teaching or learning.
Chim'bam, as they, like to them.
Chi'as, open or opening.
Chis'leu, rashness, confidence.
Chit'tim, those that bruise.
Chi'un, an Egyptian god, whom some think to be Saturn.
Chlo'e, green herb.
Cho-ra'zin, the secret, or here is a mystery.
Chu'shan-rish-a-tha'im, blackness of iniquities.
Chu'za, the seer or prophet.
Cl-lic'i-a, which rolls or overturns.
Clau'da, a lamentable voice.
Clau'di-a, lame.
Clem'ent, mild, good, merciful
Cle'o-phas, the whole glory.
Co-los'se, punishment, correction.
Co-ni'ah, the strength of the Lord.
Cor'inth, which is satisfied, or ornament, or beauty.
Cor-ne'li-us, of a horn.
Coz'bi, a liar, or as sliding away.
Cres'cens, growing, increasing.
Crete', carnal, fleshly.
Cris'pus, curled.
Cush, Ethiopians, black.
Cush'an, Ethiopia, blackness, heat.
Cush'i, the same.
Cy'ptus, fair, or fairness.
Cy-re'ne, a wall, coldness, or a floor.
Cy-re'ni-us, who governs.
Cy'rus, as miserable, or as heir.

DAB'BA-SHETH, flowing with honey.
  Dab'e-rath, word, thing, or a bee; submissive, obedient.
Da'gon, corn, or a fish.
Dal'ma-nu'tha, a bucket or branch.
Dal-ma'ti-a, deceitful lamps, or vain brightness.
Dam'a-ris, a little woman.
Da-mas'cus, a sack full of blood.
Dan, judgment, or he that judges.
Dan'i-el, judgment of God.
Da'ra, generation, or house of the shepherd, or of the companion.
Dar'l-us, he that informs himself.
Da'than, laws or rites.
Da'vid, well-beloved, dear.
Deb'o-rah, word, thing, or a bee.
De-cap'o-lis, a Greek word compounded of two others—*deca,* ten, and *polis,* city, because this country contained ten cities.
De'dan, their breasts, or friendship.
Ded'a-nim, the descendants of Dedan.
Del'i-lah, poor, small.
De'mas, popular.
De-me'tri-us, belonging to corn.
Der'be, a sting.
Deu'el, the knowledge of God.
Di-a'na, luminous, or perfect.
Di'bon, abundance of knowledge.
Di'bon-gad, abundance of sons, happy and powerful.
Did'y-mus, a twin, or double.
Di'mon, where it is red.
Di'nah, judgment, or who judges.
Din'ha-bah, she gives judgment.
Di-o-nys'i-us, divinely touched.
Di-ot're-phes, nourished by Jupiter.
Do'eg, who acts with uneasiness.
Dor, generation, or habitation.
Dor'cas, the female of a roebuck.
Do'than, the law, or custom.
Dru-sil'la, watered by the dew.
Du'mah, silence, or resemblance.
Du'ra, the same as Dor.

EASTER, the passover.
  E'bal, heap, collection of old age, a mass that disperses.
E'bed, a servant, or laborer.
E'bed'-me-lech, the king's servant.
Eb-en-e'zer, the stone of help.
E'ber, one that passes, or anger.
E-bi'a-saph, a father that gathers together, or adds.
Ed, witness.
E'den, pleasure, or delight.
E'dom, red, earthy, or of blood.
Ed're-i, a very great mass or cloud
Eg'lah, heifer, chariot, round.
Eg'la-im, drops of the sea.
Eg'lon, the same as Eglah.
E'gypt, that troubles or oppresses.
E'hud, he that praises.
Ek'ron, barrenness, torn away.

EL

E'lah, an oak, a curse, perjury.
E'lam, a young man, a virgin.
E'lath, a hind, strength, an oak.
El-beth'el, the God of Bethel.
El'dad, favored of God, love of God.
E-le-a'leh, burnt-offering of God.
E-le-a'zar, help of God, court of God.
El-e-lo'he Is'ra-el, God the God of Israel.
El-ha'nan, grace, gift, mercy of God.
E'li, the offering or lifting up.
E'li, Eli, my God, my God.
E-li'ab, God is my father, or God of the father.
E-li'a-da, knowledge of God.
E-li-a'kim, resurrection of God.
E-li'am, the people of God.
E-li'as. See Elijah.
E-li'a-shib, the God of conversion.
E-li'a-thah, thou art my God.
E-li-e'zer, help, or court of my God.
E-li-ho'reph, god of winter or youth.
E-li'hu, he is my God himself.
E-li'hud, God is my praise.
E-li'jah, God the Lord, the strong Lord.
El'i-ka, pelican of God.
E'lim, the rams, the strong, or stags.
E-lim'e-lech, my God is king.
E-li-oe'na-i, toward him are mine eyes, or toward him are my fountains.
E-liph'a-let, the God of deliverance.
E-liph'az, the endeavor of God.
E-lis'a-beth, the oath of God.
E-li'sha, salvation of God.
E-li'shah, it is God, the Lamb of God, God that gives help.
E-lish'a-mah, God hearing.
E-lish'e-ba. See Elisabeth.
E-li-shu'a, God is my salvation.
E-li'zur, God is my strength, my rock, or rock of God.
El'ka-nah, God the zealous, or the reed of God.
El'mo-dam, the God of measure.
El'na-than, God hath given, or the gift or God.
E'lon, oak, grove, or strong.
E'lul, cry, or outcry.
E-lu'za-i, God is my strength.
El'y-mas, a magician.
E'mims, fears, terrors, formidable, or people.
Em'ma-us, people despised, or obscure.
Em'mor, an ass.
En'dor, fountain, eye of generation, or habitation.
E-ne'as, laudable.
En-eg-la'im, eye of the calves.
En'ge-di, eye of the goat, or of happiness.
En-mish'pat, fountain of judgment.
E'noch, dedicated, or disciplined.
E'non, cloud, or mass of darkness.
Enos, mortal man, sick, despaired of, forgetful.
En-ro'gel, the fuller's fountain.
En'she-mesh, fountain, or eye of the sun.
Ep'a-phras, covered with foam.
E-paph-ro-di'tus, agreeable, handsome.
E-pen'e-tus, laudable, worthy of praise.
E'phah, weary, tired.
E-phes-dam'mim, effusion of blood.
Eph'e-sus, desirable.
Eph'pha-tha, be opened.
E'phra-im, that brings fruit.
Eph'ra-tah, abundance, or bearing fruit.
Eph'rath, the same as Ephratah.

GE

E'phron, dust.
E-pi-cu're-an, who gives assistance.
Er, watch, or enemy.
E-ras'tus, lovely, amiable.
E'rech, length, health, or physic.
E-sai-a's. See Isaiah.
E'sar-had-don, that closes the point.
E'sau, he that acts or finishes.
E'sek, contention.
Esh'ba-al, the fire of the idol.
Esh'col, bunch of grapes.
Esh'ta-ol, stout, strong woman.
Esh-tem'o-a, the bosom of a woman.
Es'li, near me, or he who separates.
Es'rom, dart of joy, division of the song.
Es'ther, secret, hidden.
E'tam, their bird, or covering.
E'tham, their strength, their sign.
E'than, strong, or the gift of the island.
Eth'a-nim, strong, valiant.
Eth'ba-al, toward the idol, or with Baal.
E-thi-o'pi-a, blackness, heat.
Eu-bu'lus, prudent, good counselor.
Eu-ni'ce, good victory.
Eu-o'di-as, sweet scent.
Eu-phra'tes, that makes fruitful.
Eu'ty-chus, happy, fortunate.
Eve, living, enlivening.
E'vil-me-ro'dach, the fool of Merodach, the fool grinds bitterly.
E-ze'ki-el, the strength of God.
E'zel, going abroad, or walk.
E'zi-on-ge'ber, the wood of the man.
Ez'ra, help, or court.

F E'LIX, happy, or prosperous.
Fes'tus, festival, or joyful.
For-tu-na'tus, lucky, or fortunate.

G A'AL, contempt or abomination.
Ga'ash, tempest, commotion.
Gab'ba-tha, high, elevated.
Ga'bri-el, God is my strength.
Gad, a band, happy.
Gad'a-renes, surrounded, walled.
Gad'di, my happiness.
Gad'di-el, goat of God.
Ga'ius, lord, an earthy man.
Ga-la'ti-a, white, the color of milk.
Gal-ba'num, a sort of gum, or sweet spice.
Gal'e-ed, the heap of witness.
Gal'i-lee, wheel, revolution, heap.
Gal'lim, who heap up, who cover.
Gal'li-o, who sucks or lives on milk.
Ga-ma'li-el, recompense of God.
Gam'ma-dims, signify dwarfs, soldiers placed in the towers of Tyrus.
Ga'tam, their lowing.
Gath, a press.
Gath-rim'mon, the exalted press.
Ga'za, strong, or a goat.
Ge'ba, a hill or cup.
Ge'bal, bound, or limit.
Ge'bim, grasshoppers, or height.
Ged-a-li'ah, God is my greatness.
Ge-ha'zi, valley of sight.
Gem-a-ri'ah, accomplishment of the Lord.
Gen-nes'a-ret, garden of the prince.
Ge-nu'bath, theft, robbery.
Ge'ra, pilgrimage, combat dispute.
Ge'rah, twentieth part of a shekel.
Ge'rar. See Gera.
Ger-ge-senes', those who come from pilgrimage or fight.

GE | IP

Ger'i-zim, cutters.
Ger'shom, a stranger there.
Ger'shon, his banishment, or the change of pilgrimage.
Ge'shur, the sight of the valley.
Ge'ther, the vale of trial.
Geth-sem'a-ne, a very fat valley.
Gi'ah, to guide, draw out, produce.
Gib'e-ah, a hill.
Gib'e-on, hill, cup, or elevation of iniquity.
Gid'e-on, he that bruises and breaks, or cutting off iniquity.
Gid-e-o'ni, the same as Gideon.
Gi'hon, valley of grace.
Gil'bo-a, revolution of inquiry.
Gil'e-ad, the heap, or mass of testimony.
Gil'gal, wheel, revolution, heap.
Gi'loh, he that rejoices, that overturns.
Gir'ga-shite, who arrives from pilgrimage.
Git'ute, a wine press.
Gob, cistern, or grasshopper.
Gog, roof, or covering.
Go'lan, passage, or revolution.
Gol'go-tha, an heap of skulls.
Go-li'ath, passage, revolution, heap.
Go'mer, to finish, complete.
Go-mor'rah, rebellious people.
Go'shen, approaching, drawing near.
Go'zan, fleece, pasture, who nourisheth the body.
Gre-ci'a, the country of the Greeks.
Gur, the young of a beast; dwelling, assembly, or fear.

HAB'AK-KUK, he that embraces.
Hach-al'iah, who waits for the Lord.
Hach'i-lah, my hope is in her.
Ha'dad, joy, noise, clamor.
Had-ad-e'zer, beauty of assistance.
Ha'dad-rim'mon, cry of the exalted, the invocation to the god Rimmon.
Ha-das'sah, a myrtle, or joy.
Ha-do'ram, their beauty, or their power.
Ha'drach, point, joy of tenderness.
Ha'gar, a stranger, or that fears.
Hag'ga-i, feast, solemnity.
Hag'gith, rejoicing.
Hal-le-lu'iah, praise the Lord.
Ham, hot, heat, or brown.
Ha'man, noise, tumult.
Ha'math, anger, heat, or wall.
Ham-med'a-tha, he that troubles the law.
Ha'mon-gog, the multitude of Gog.
Ha'mor, an ass, clay, or wine.
Ham'u-tal, the shadow of his seat.
Ha-nam'e-el, the grace that comes from God, the gift of God.
Ha-nan'e-el, grace, gift of God.
Han'a-ni, my grace, my mercy.
Han-a-ni'ah, grace, mercy, or gift of the Lord.
Han'nah, gracious, merciful, he that gives.
Han'och, dedicated.
Ha'num, gracious, merciful.
Ha'ran, mountainous country.
Har'ran. See Charran.
Har-bo'nah, his destruction, or his sword.
Ha'rod, astonishment, fear.
Har'o-seth, agriculture, silence.
Hash-mo'nah, diligence, or enumeration embassy, or present.
Ha'tach, he that strikes.
Hav'i-lah, that suffers pain, that brings forth.
Ha'voth-ja-ir, the villages that enlighten.

Haz'a-el, that sees God.
Ha'zar-ma'veth, dwelling of death.
Ha'zel-el-po'ni, sorrow of countenance.
Haz-e'roth, villages, or hamlets.
Ha'zor, court, or hay.
He'ber, one that passes, or anger.
He'brews, the descendants of Heber.
He'bron, society, friendship.
Heg'a-i, or Hege, meditation, word, separation, or groaning.
He'lam, their army, their trouble.
Hel'bon, milk, or fatness.
Hel'da-i, the world.
He'li, ascending, or climbing up.
Hel'kath-haz'zu-rim, the field of strong men
He'man, their trouble, or tumult.
He'man, much or in great number.
Hen, grace, quiet, or rest.
Heph'zi-bah, my delight is in her.
Her'mes, Mercury, grain, or refuge.
Her-mog'e-nes, begotten of Mercury.
Her'mon, anathema, destruction.
Her'od, the glory of the skin
He-ro'di-as, the wife of Herod.
He-ro'di-on, the song of Juno.
Hesh'bon, invention, industry.
Heth, trembling, or fear.
Heth'lon, fearful dwelling.
Hez-e-ki'ah, strength of the Lord.
Hez'ron, the dart of joy, or the division of the song.
Hid'de-kel, sharp voice or sound.
Hi'el, God lives, the life of God.
Hi-e-rap'o-lis, holy city.
Hig-ga'ion, meditation, consideration.
Hil-ki'ah, God is my portion.
Hil'lel, he that praises.
Hin'nom, there they are.
Hi'ram, exaltation of life.
Hit'tite, who is broken, or fears.
Hi'vites, wicked, wickedness.
Ho'bab, favored and beloved.
Ho'bab, love, friendship, or secrecy.
Hog'lah, his festival, or dance.
Hoph'ni, he that covers, or my fist.
Hor, who conceives, or shows.
Ho'reb, desert, solitude, destruction.
Hor-ha-gid'gad, the hill of felicity.
Hor'mah, devoted or consecrated to God, utter destruction.
Ho-ro-na'im, anger, or raging.
Hor'o-nite, anger, fury, liberty.
Ho-se'a, and Hoshea, saviour, or safety.
Hul, pain, infirmity.
Hul'dah, the world.
Hur, liberty, whiteness.
Hu'shai, their haste, their sensuality, their silence.
Huz'zab, molten.
Hy-men-e'us, nuptial, or the god of marriage.

I B'AHR, election, or he that is chosen.
Ich'a-bod, where is the glory?
I-co'ni-um, I come, the name of a city.
Id'do, his hand, power, or praise.
Id-u-me'a, red, earthy, bloody.
Ig-da-li'a, the greatness of the Lord.
I'jon, look, eye, fountain
Il-lyr'i-cum, joy, rejoicing.
Im'lah, plenitude, or circumcision.
Im-man'u-el, God with us.
In'di-a, praise, law.
Iph-e-de'iah, redemption of the Lord.

IR

I'ra, city, watch, or spoil.
I'rad, wild ass, heap of descents.
I-ri'jah, the fear of the Lord.
I'saac, laughter.
I-sai'ah, the salvation of the Lord.
Is'cah, he that anoints.
Is-cari-ot, a man of murder.
Ish'bak, who is empty or exhausts.
Ish'bi-be'nob, he that sits in the prophecy.
Ish'bo-sheth, a man of shame.
Ish'ma-el, God that hears.
Is'ra-el, who prevails with God.
Is'sa-char, reward, or recompense.
It-a'ly, a Latin word, that has its original from *vitulus*, or *vitula*, because this country abounded in calves and heifers. Others say it is taken from *Italus*, a king.
Ith'a-mar, island of the palm-tree.
Ith'i-el, sign, or coming of God.
Ith're-am, excellence of the people.
It-u-re'a, which is guarded.
I'vah, iniquity.

J A-A'LAM, who is hidden.
Ja-az-a-ni'ah, whom the Lord will hear.
Ja'bal, which glides away.
Jab'bok, evacuation, or dissipation.
Jab'esh, dryness, confusion, shame.
Ja'bez, sorrow, or trouble.
Ja'bin, he that understands.
Jab'ne-el, building of God.
Ja'chin, he that strengthens and makes steadfast.
Ja'cob, that supplants, or undermines.
Ja'el, he that ascends, or a kid.
Jah, the everlasting.
Ja'haz, quarrel, dispute.
Ja-ha'za, the same.
Ja'ir, my light, who diffuses light.
Ja'i-rus, the same.
Jam'bres, poverty, bitter, a rebel.
James, the same as Jacob.
Jan'na, who speaks, or answers.
Jan'nes, the same.
Ja'pheth, he that persuades.
Japh'i-a, which enlightens, or appears.
Ja'reb, a revenger.
Ja'red, he that descends, or rules.
Ja'sher, righteous.
Ja'son, he that cures.
Ja'van, he that deceives, or makes sorrowful.
Ja'zer, assistance, or he that helps.
Je'bus, which treads under foot.
Jec-o-ni-ah, preparation of the Lord.
Jed'i-dah, well-beloved, amiable.
Jed-i-di'ah, beloved of the Lord.
Jed-u'thun, his law, or who gives praise.
Je'gar-sa-ha-du'tha, the heap of witness.
Je-ho'a-haz, possession of the Lord.
Je-ho'ash, the fire of the Lord.
Je-hoi'a-chin, strength of the Lord.
Je-hoi'a-da, knowledge of the Lord.
Je-hoi'a-kim, resurrection of the Lord.
Je-hon'a-dab. See Jonadab.
Je-ho'ram, exaltation of the Lord.
Je-hosh'a-phat, God judges.
Je-ho'vah, self-subsisting.
Je-ho'vah-ji'reh, the Lord will see or provide.
Je-ho'vah-ni'ssi, the Lord my banner.
Je-ho'vah-sha'lom, the Lord send peace.
Je-ho'vah-sham'mah, the Lord is there.
Je-ho'vah-tsid-ke-nu, the Lord our righteousness.
Je'hu, himself, who exists.

JU

Je-hu-di'jah, the praise of the Lord.
Je-mi'ma, handsome as the day.
Jeph'thah, he that opens.
Je-phun'neh, he that beholds.
Je'rah, the moon, or month.
Je-rahm'e-el, mercy of God.
Jer-e-mi'ah, exaltation of the Lord.
Jer'i-cho, his moon, or month.
Jer'i-moth, he that fears or rejects death.
Jer-o-bo'am, he that opposes the people.
Je-rub'ba-al, he that defends Baal, let Baal defend his cause.
Je-rub'be-sheth, let the idol of confusion defend itself.
Je-ru'sa-lem, vision of peace.
Je-ru'sha, exiled, or banished.
Jesh'i-mon, solitude or desolation.
Jesh'u-a, a saviour.
Jesh'u-run, upright, or righteous.
Jes'se, to be, or who is.
Jes'u-i, who is equal, or flat country.
Jes'us, Saviour.
Je'ther, he that excels.
Jeth'ro, his excellence, or posterity.
Je'tur, order, succession, mountainous.
Je'ush, he that is devoured.
Jew. See Judah.
Jez'e-bel, island of the habitation.
Jez-ra-hi'ah, the Lord arises.
Jez're-el, seed of God, the brightness of the Lord.
Jid'laph, he that distills water.
Jo'ab, paternity, voluntary.
Jo'ah, fraternity, brother of the Lord.
Jo-an'na, grace or gift of the Lord.
Jo'ash, who despairs, or burns.
Job, he that weeps, or cries.
Joch'e-bed, glorious, honorable.
Jo'el, he that wills or commands.
Jo-e'zer, he that aids or assists.
Jo'ha, who enlivens and gives life.
Jo-ha'nan, who is liberal or merciful.
John, the grace or mercy of the Lord.
Jok'shan, hard or difficult.
Jok'tan, small, dispute, contention.
Jon'a-dab, who acts in good earnest.
Jo'nah, or Jonas, a dove, or he that oppresses.
Jon'a-than, given of God.
Jop'pa, beauty or comeliness.
Jo'ram, to cast, elevated.
Jor'dan, the river of judgment.
Jo'rim, he that exalts the Lord.
Jos'e, raised, or who pardons.
Jo'seph, increase or addition.
Jo'ses, the same with Jose.
Josh'u-a, the Lord, the Saviour.
Jo-si'ah, the Lord burns, the fire of the Lord.
Jo'tham, the perfection of the Lord.
Ju'bal, he that runs.
Ju'bi-lee, a feast of the Jews, kept every fiftieth year; in Hebrew, *Jobel*, which some say signifies *a ram's horn*, by which the Jubilee year was proclaimed. Others say that *Jobal* is another form of the word *Jubal*, which formerly signified, as they say, *to play upon instruments*. Others are of opinion that it comes from the verb *Hobil*, to *bring* or *call back*, as then every thing was restored to its first possessor.
Ju'dah, the praise of the Lord.
Ju'das, the same.
Ju'li-a, downy, soft and tender hair.
Ju'li-as, the same.
Ju'ni-a, youth.

JU

Ju'pi-ter, the father that helpeth.
Jus'tus, just or upright.

K AB'ZE-EL, the congregation of God.
Ka'desh, holy, or holiness.
Ka-desh-bar-ne-a, holiness of an inconstant
Ked'ar, blackness, sorrow.   [son.
Ke'de-moth, oriental.
Ked e-moth, antiquity, old age.
Kei'lah, she that divides or cuts.
Ke-mu'el, God is risen.
Ke naz, this nest, this lamentation.
Ken'ites, possession or purchase.
Ke'ren-hap puch, the horn or child of beauty.
Ke'ri-oth, the cities, the callings.
Ke-tu'rah, be that makes the incense, to
fume.
Ke-zi'a, superficies, an angle, cassia.
Kez'iz, end, extremity.
Kib'roth-hat-ta'a-vah, the graves of lust.
Kid'ron, obscurity, obscure.
Kir, a city, wall, or meeting.
Kir-har'e-seth, the city of the sun.
Kir'jath-a'im, the two cities, calling, or
meetings.
Kir'jath, city, vocation, lesson.
Kir jath-ar'ba, the city of four.
Kir'jath-a'rim, city of those who watch.
Kir jath-ba al, the city of Baal.
Kir'jath-je-a'rim, the city of woods.
Kir'jath-san'nah, the city of enmity.
Kir'jath-seph'er, the city of letters.
Kish, hard, difficult, or straw forage.
Kit'tim, they that bruise, or gold or color-
Ko'hath, congregation, wrinkle.   [ing.
Ko'rah, bald, frozen, icy.

L A'BAN, white, or a brick.
La'chish, she walks, she goes.
Lah'mi, my bread, or my war.
La'ish, a lion.
La' mech, poor, made low.
La-o-di-ce'a, just people.
Lap'i-doth, enlightened, or lamps.
Laz'a-rus, assistance of God.
Le'ah, weary, or tired.
Leb'a-non, white, or incense.
Leb-be'us, a man of heart.
Le'ha-bim, flames, or inflamed.
Le'hi, jaw-bone.
Lem'u-el, God with them or him.
Le'vi, who is held and associated.
Lib'nah, white, whiteness.
Lib'ni, the same.
Lib'y-a, the heart of the sea.
Li'nus, nets.
Lo-am'mi, not my people.
Lo'is, better.
Lo-ru'ha-mah, not having obtained mercy, not
pitied.
Lot, wrapt up, hidden, covered.
Lu'cas, Lucius, Luke, luminous.
Lu'ci-fer, bringing light.
Luz, separation, departure.
Lyc-a-o'ni-a, she-wolf.
Ly'sa-ni-as that drives away sorrow.
Lys'tra, that dissolves or disperses.

M A'A-CHAH, to squeeze.
Ma-a-sei'ah, work of the Lord.
Ma-e-do'ni-a, adoration, prostration.
Ma'chir, he that sells, or knows.
Mach-pe'lah, double.
Mag'da-la, tower, or greatness.

ME

Mag-da'lene, elevated, magnificence.
Ma gog, roof, or that covers.
Ma gor-mis sa-bib, fear round about.
Ma-hal-a-le'el, he that praises God.
Ma'ha-lath, melodious song.
Ma-ha-na'im, two fields, or armies.
Ma'her-shal'al-hash'-baz, making speed to
the spoil, he hasteneth the prey.
Mah'lah. See Mahalath.
Mah'lon, song, or infirmity.
Mak-ke'dah, adoration, prostration.
Mal'cham, their king.
Mal-chi-shu'a, my king is a saviour.
Mal'chus, king, or kingdom.
Mam'mon, riches.
Mam're, rebellious, or bitter.
Man'a-en, a comforter.
Ma-nas'seh, forgetfulness, he that is forgot-
ten.
Ma-no'ah, rest, or a present.
Ma'on, house, habitation.
Ma'ra, bitter, bitterness.
Ma'rah, the same.
Mar'cus, polite, shining.
Mark, the same.
Mars-hill, the place where the celebrated
judges of Athens held their supreme coun-
cil.
Mar'tha, who becomes bitter.
Ma'ry. See Miriam.
Mas're-kah, whistling, or hissing.
Mas'sah, temptation.
Mat'ri, rain, or prison.
Mat'tan, gift, or the rains.
Mat-ta-thi'as, the gift of the Lord.
Mat'that, gift, or he that gives.
Matth'ew, given.
Mat-thi'as. See Mattathias.
Maz-za'roth, the twelve signs.
Me'dad, he that measures, the water of love.
Me'dan, judgment, process.
Me'di-a, a measure, habit, covering.
Me-gid'do, his precious fruit.
Me-gid'don, the same.
Me-het-a-bel, how good is God.
Me-hu'ja-el, who proclaims God.
Mel'chi, my king, my counsel.
Mel-chiz'e-dek, king of justice.
Mel'i-ta, affording honey.
Mem'phis, by the mouth.
Me-mu'can, impoverished, or to prepare, or
certain, true.
Men'a-hem, comforter, who conducts them,
preparation of heat.
Me-ne', who reckons, or is counted.
Me-phib'o-sheth, out of my mouth proceeds
reproach.
Me'rab, he that fights or disputes.
Mer-a'ri, bitter, to provoke.
Mer-cu'ri-us, an orator, an interpreter.
Mer'i-bah, dispute, quarrel.
Me-rib-ba-al, rebellion, he that resists Baal.
Me-ro'dach, bitter contrition.
Mer'o-dach-bal-a-dan, who creates contri-
tion, the son of death.
Me'rom, eminences, elevations.
Me'roz, secret, or leanness.
Me'shach, that draws with force.
Me'shech, who is drawn by force.
Mesh-el-e-mi'ah, peace, or perfection.
Mes-o-po-ta'mi-a, between two rivers.
Mes-si'ah, anointed.
Me'theg-am'mah, bridle of bondage.
Me-thu'sa-el, who demands his death.

ME

Me-thu'se-lah, he has sent his death.
Mi'cah, poor, humb'e
Mi-cai'ah, who is like .o God ?
Mi-chai'ah, Michael, the same.
Mi'chal, who is perfect ?
Mich'mash, he that strikes.
Mid'i-an, judgment, covering, habit.
Mig'ron, fear, farm, throat.
Mil'cah, queen.
Mil'com, their king.
Mi-le'tum, red, scarlet.
Mil'lo, fullness, plenitude, repletio ı.
Min'ni, reckoned, prepared.
Min'nith, counted, prepared.
Mir'i-am, exalted, bitterness of the sea.
Mish'a-el, who is asked for or lent.
Mis're-photh-ma'im, the burnings of the waters.
Mit-y-le'ne, purity, cleansing, press.
Mi'zar, little.
Miz'pah, a sentinel, speculation.
Miz'peth, the same.
Miz ra-im, tribulations.
Mna son, a diligent seeker, an exhorter.
Mo'ab, of his father.
Mol'a-dah, birth, generation.
Mo'lech, or Moloch, king.
Mor'de-cai, contrition, bitter, bruising.
Mo-ri'ah, bitterness of the Lord.
Mo-se'roth, erudition, discipline.
Mo'ses, taken out of the water.
Mu'shi, he that touches, that withdraws or takes away.
My'ra, I flow, pour out, weep.
Mys'ia, criminal, abominable.

NA'A-MAN, beautiful, agreeable.
Na-ash'on, that foretells, that conjectures.
Na'bal, fool, or senseless.
Na'both, words, prophecies.
Na'dab, free and voluntary gift.
Nag'ge, brightness.
Na-har'i, my nostrils, hot, anger.
Na'hash, snake or serpent.
Na'hor, hoarse, dry, hot.
Na'hum, comforter, penitent.
Na'in, beauty, pleasantness.
Nai oth, beauties, or habitations.
Na'o-mi, beautiful, agreeable.
Na'phish, the soul, he that rests, refreshes himself, or respires.
Naph'ta-li, that struggles or fights.
Nar-cis'sus, astonishment, stupidity.
Na'than, who gives, or is given.
Na-than'a-el, the gift of God.
Na'than-me'lech, the gift of the King.
Na'um. See Nahum.
Naz-a-rene', kept, or flower.
Naz'a-reth, separated, guarded, flourishing.
Ne-ap'olis, the new city.
Ne-bai'oth, words, prophecies, fruits.
Ne'bat, that beholds.
Ne'bo, that speaks or prophesies.
Ne-bu-chad-nez'zar, tears and groans, or judgment.
Ne-bu-zar'a-dan, fruit or prophecies of judgment.
Ne'cho, lame, beaten.
Ne-hel'a-mite, dreamer, vale, brook.
Ne-he-mi'ah, consolation, repentance of the Lord.
Ne-hush'ta, snake, soothsayer.

PA

Ne-hush'tan, of brass or copper.
Ne?, lamp, or new tilled land.
Ne re-us, the same.
Ne ri, my light.
Ne-ri'ah, light, lamp of the Lord.
Ne-than'e-el. See Nathanael.
Neth-a-ni'ah, the gift of the Lord.
Neth'i-nims, given or offered.
Nib'haz, that fructifies, that produces vision.
Ni-ca'nor, a conqueror, victorious.
Nic-o-de'mus, innocent blood.
Nic-o-la'i-tans, the followers of Nicholas.
Nic'o-las, victory of the people.
Ni-cop'o-lis, the city of victory.
Nig'er, black.
Nim'rim, leopard, bitterness.
Nim'rod, rebellion, him that rules.
Nim'shi, rescued from danger.
Nin'e-veh, handsome, agreeable.
Ni'san, flight, or standard proof.
Nis'roch, flight, proof, temptation, tender, delicate.
No, stirring up, a forbidding.
No-a-di'ah, witness, ornament of the Lord.
No'ah, repose, rest, consolation.
No'ah, that quavers or totters, Zelophehad's daughter.
Nob, discourse, prophecy.
No'bah, that barks or yelps.
Nod, vagabond.
Noph, honeycomb, or sieve, or that drops.
Nun, son, durable and eternal.
Nym'phas, spouse or bridegroom.

O-BA-DI'AH, servant of the Lord.
O'bal, inconvenience of old age.
O'bed, a servant.
O'bed-e'dom, the slave of Edom.
O'bil, that weeps, or who deserves to be bewailed.
Oc'ran, disturber, that disorders.
O'ded, to sustain, hold or lift up.
Og, a cake, bread baked in ashes.
O'hel, tent, tabernacle, brightness.
O-lym'pas, heavenly.
O'mar, he that speaks, or bitter.
O'me-ga, the last letter of the Greek alphabet.
Om'ri, sheaf or bundle of corn.
On, pain, force, iniquity.
O'nan, power, strength, iniquity.
O-nes'i-mus, profitable, useful.
On-e-siph'o-rus, who brings profit.
O'phel, a tower or elevated place.
O'phir, ashes.
Oph'rah, dust, fawn, lead.
O'reb, a raven, sweet, or evening.
O-ri'on, a constellation.
Or'nan, that rejoices.
Or'pah, the neck or skull.
Oth'ni, my time, my hour.
Oth'ni-el, the hour of God.
O'zem, that fasts, their eagerness.
O-zi'as, strength from the Lord.

PA'A-RAI, opening.
Pa'dan-a'ram, Syria, of a pair or two, Mesopotamia, because situated between two rivers.
Pa'gi-el, prevention of God, prayer of God.
Pal-es-ti'na, which is covered, watered, or brings an causes ruin.
Pal'ti, deliverance, flight.
Pam-phyl'ia a nation made up of every tribe

23

PA

Pa'phos, which boils, or which is very hot.
Pa'ran, beauty, glory, ornament.
Par'bar, a gate or building belonging to the temple.
Par'me-nas, that abides, or is permanent.
Pa'rosh, a flea, the fruit of a moth.
Par-shan'da-tha, the revelation of corporeal impurities.
Par'thi-ans, horsemen.
Par'u-ah, flourishing, or that flies away.
Pash'ur, that extends or multiplies the whole, or whiteness.
Pat'a-ra, which is trod under foot.
Path'ros, mouthful of dew, persuasion, or dilation of ruin.
Pat'mos, mortal.
Pat'ro-bas, paternal, that pursues the steps of his father.
Pa'u, that cries aloud, that appears.
Paul, small, little.
Paul'us, the same.
Ped'ah-zur, saviour, strong and powerful, or stone of redemption.
Pe-dai'ah, redemption of the Lord.
Pe'kah, he that opens, or is at liberty.
Pek-a-hi'ah, it is the Lord that opens.
Pel-a-ti'ah, let the Lord deliver, deliverance of the Lord.
Pe'leg, division.
Pe'leth-ites, judges, or destroyers.
Pe-ni'el, face or vision of God, that sees God.
Pen'in-nah, pearl, precious stone, or the face.
Pe-nu'el. See Peniel.
Pe'or, hole, opening.
Per'ga, very earthy.
Per'ga-mos, height, elevation.
Per'iz-zites, a name given to those who dwell in villages.
Per'si-a, that cuts, or divides, or a nail, gryphon, or horseman.
Per'sis, the same.
Pe'ter, a rock or stone.
Pe-thu'el, mouth of God, persuasion of God.
Pha'lec. See Peleg.
Phal'lu, admirable, hidden.
Phal'ti, deliverance, flight.
Pha-nu'el, face or vision of God.
Pha'ra-oh, that disperses, that spoils.
Pha'rez, division, rupture.
Phar'par, that produces fruit, the fall of the bull.
Phe'be, shining, pure.
Phe-ni'ce, red, purple.
Phi'col, the mouth of all, or every tongue.
Phil-a-del'phi-a, love of a brother.
Phi-le'mon, who kisses.
Phi-le'tus, amiable, who is beloved.
Phil'ip, warlike, a lover of horses.
Phi-lip'pi, the same.
Phil-is'ti-a, the country of the Philistines.
Phi-lis'tines, those that dwell in villages.
Phi-lol'o-gus, a lover of letters, or of the word.
Phin'e-has, aspect, face of trust, or protection.
Phle'gon, zealous, burning.
Phryg'i-a, dry, barren.
Phu'rah, that bears fruit, or grows.
Phy-gel'lus, fugitive.
Pi-ha-hi'roth, the mouth, the pass of Hiroth.
Pi'late, who is armed with a dart.
Pi'non, pearl, gem, that beholds.
Pir'a-thon, his dissipation, deprivation, his rupture.

RE

Pis'gah, hill, eminence, fortress.
Pi-sid'i-a, pitch, pitchy.
Pi'son, changing, extension of the mouth.
Pi'thom, their mouthful or bit, a dilation of the mouth.
Pi'thon, his mouth, his persuasion.
Pon'ti-us, marine, belonging to the sea.
Pon'tus, the sea.
Por'a-tha, fruitful.
Pot'i-phar, bull of Africa, a fat bull.
Po-thi'Ye-rah, that scatters or demolishes the f.
Pris'ca, ancient.
Pris-cil'la, the same.
Proch'o-rus, he that presides over the choirs.
Pub'li-us, common.
Pu'dens, shamefacedness.
Pul, bean, or destruction.
Pun'on, precious stone, or that beholds.
Pur, lot.
Pu-te'o-li, a city in Campania.
Pu'ti-el, God is my fatness.

QUAR'TUS, the fourth.

RA'A-MAH, greatness, thunder, some sort of evil.
Rab'bah, great, powerful, contentious, disputative.
Rab'mag, who overthrows, or destroys a multitude.
Rab'-sa-ris, grand-master of the eunuchs.
Rab'sha-keh, cup-bearer of the prince.
Ra'chal, injurious, or perfumer.
Ra'chel, sheep.
Rag'au, a friend, a neighbor.
Ra-gu'el, shepherd, or friend of God.
Ra'hab, proud, quarrelsome, a name given to Egypt.
Ra'hab, large, extended, the name of a woman.
Rak'kath, empty, temple of the head.
Rak'kon, vain, void, mountain of lamentations and tears.
Ram, elevated, sublime.
Ra'mah, the same.
Ra'math, raised, lofty.
Ra-math-a'im-zoph'im, watch-tower.
Ra-math-le'hi, elevation of the jaw-bone.
Ra-me'ses, thunder.
Ra'moth, eminences, high places.
Ra'pha, relaxation, or physic.
Ra'phu, cured, comforted.
Re'ba, the fourth, a square, that lies or stoops down.
Re-bek'ah, fat, fattened, a quarrel appeased.
Re'chab, square, chariot, a team of horses.
Re'gem, that stones, or is stoned.
Re-gem'me-lech, he that stones the king.
Re-ha-bi'ah, breadth, extent.
Re'hab, breadth, space, extent.
Re-ho-bo'am, who sets the people at liberty
Re-ho'both, spaces, places.
Re'hum, merciful, compassionate.
Re i, my shepherd, my companion, my friend.
Rem-a-li'ah, the exaltation of the Lord.
Rem'mon, greatness, elevation; or a pomegranate-tree.
Rem'phan, the name of an idol.
Re'pha el, the physic or medicine of God.
Reph'a-im, giant, physician, relaxed.
Reph-i-dim, beds, or places of rest.

RE

Re'sen, a bridle or bit.
Re-u', his friend, his shepherd, his misfortune.
Reu'ben, who sees the son, the vision of the son.
Reu'el, the shepherd or friend of God.
Reu'mah, lofty, sublime.
Rez'in, voluntary, good-will.
Rez'on, lean, small, secret, prince.
Rhe'gi-um, rupture, fracture.
Rhe'sa, will, course.
Rho'da, a rose.
Rhodes, the same.
Rib'lah, quarrel, greatness to him.
Rim'mon, exalted, pomegranate.
Ri'phath, remedy, medicine, release, pardon.
Ris'sah, watering, distillation.
Riz'pah, bed, extension, coal, fire-stone.
Ro'man-ti-ce'zer, exaltation of help.
Ro'man, strong, powerful.
Rome, strength, power.
Rosh, the head, top, or beginning.
Ru'fus, red.
Ru'ha-mah, having obtained mercy.
Ru'mah, exalted, sublime, rejected.
Ruth, drunk, satisfied.

SA-BE'ANS, captivity, conversion, old age.
Sab'te-cha, that surrounds, that causes wounding.
Sa'doc, just, justified.
Sa'lah, mission, sending.
Sal'a-mis, shaken, test, beaten.
Sa-la'thi-el, I have asked of God, the loan of God.
Sa'lem, complete, perfect, peace.
Sa'lim. See Shalim.
Sal'mon, peaceable, perfect, he that rewards.
Sal-mo'ne, a city.
Sa-lo'ne, the same as Salmon.
Sa-ma'ri-a, his lees, his prison, his throne, his diamond.
Sam'lah, his raiment, his left hand, his astonishment.
Sa'mos, full of gravel.
Sa-mo-thra'ci-a, a name given to an island possessed by the Samians and Thracians.
Sam'son, his sun, his service, hear the second time.
Sam'u-el, heard of God, asked of God.
San-bal'lat, bush in secret, enemy in secret.
Saph, rushes, sea-moss.
Saph'ir, a city.
Sap-phi'ra, that relates, or tells.
Sa'rah, lady, princess ; princess of the multitude.
Sa'ra-i, my lady, my princess.
Sar'dis, prince of joy.
Sa-rep'ta, a goldsmith's shop.
Sar'gon, who takes away protection.
Sa'ron. See Sharon.
Sar-se'chim, master of the wardrobe.
Sa'ruch, branch, layer, twining.
Sa'tan, contrary, adversary, enemy, accuser.
Saul', demanded, lent, ditch, hell.
Sce'va, disposed, prepared.
Scyth'i-an, tanner, leather-dresser.
Se'ba, a drunkard, that turns.
Se'bat, twig, sceptre, tribe.
Se'gub, fortified, raised.
Se'ir, hairy, goat, demon, tempest.
Se'lah, the end, a pause.
Se-leu'ci-a, shaken or beaten by the waves.

SH

Sem'e-i, hearing, obeying.
Sen'eh, bush.
Sen-na-che'rib, bush of the destruction of the sword.
Seph-ar-va'im, the two books, the two scribes.
Se'rah, lady of scent, the song, the morning, the morning star.
Se-ra-i'ah, prince of the Lord.
Se'rug, branch, layer, twining.
Seth, put, or who puts.
Sha-al'bim, that beholds the heart.
Sha-a-ra'im, gates, valuation, hairs.
Sha-ash'gaz, he that presses the fleece, that shears the sheep.
Sha'drach, tender, nipple.
Sha'lim, fox, fist, path.
Shal'i-sha, three, the third, prince or captain.
Shal'lum, perfect, agreeable.
Shal'man, peaceable, perfect, that rewards.
Shal-ma-ne'zer, peace, tied, or chained, perfection and retribution.
Sham'gar, named a stranger, he is here a stranger.
Sham'huth, desolation, destruction.
Sha'mir, prison, bush, lees, thorn.
Sham'mah, loss, desolation, astonishment.
Sham-mu'ah, he that is heard, he that is obeyed.
Sha'phan, rabbit, wild rat, their lip, the brink.
Sha'phat, that judges.
Shar'a-i, my lord, my prince, my song.
Sha-re'zer, overseer of the treasury, or of the storehouse.
Shar'on, his plain, his song.
Sha'shak, a bag of linen, or the sixth bag.
Sha'veh, the plain, that puts or maketh equality.
She-al'ti-el, I have asked of God.
She-a-ri'ah, gate of the Lord, tempest of the Lord.
She'ar-ja'shub, the remnant shall return.
She'ba, captivity, conversion, old age.
Sheb-a-ni'ah, the Lord that converts, or recalls from captivity.
Sheb'na, who rests himself, who is now captive.
She'chem, part, portion, back, early in the morning.
Shed'e-ur, field, pap, all-mighty, destroyer of fire.
She'lah, that breaks, that unties, that undresses.
Shel-e-mi'ah, God is my perfection, my happiness, my peace.
She'leph, who draws out.
Shel'o-mith, my peace, my happiness, my recompense.
She-lu'mi-el, peace of God, God is my happiness.
Shem, name, renown.
Shem-a-i'ah, that hears, or that obeys the Lord.
Shem-a-ri'ah, God is my guard.
Shem'e-ber, name of force, fame of the strong.
She'mer, guardian, thorn.
She-mi'da, name of knowledge that puts knowledge.
Shem'i-nith, the eighth.
She-mir'a-moth, the night of the heavens.
Shen, tooth, ivory, change.

SH

She'nir, lantern, light that sleeps.
Sheph-a-ti'ah, the Lord that judges.
She'shach, bag of flax, or linen.
Shesh-baz'zar, joy in tribulation, joy of the vintage.
She'thar-boz'na-i, that makes to rot, that seeks those who despise me.
She'va, vanity, elevation, fame, tumult.
Shib'bo-leth, burden, ear of corn.
Shi'cou, drunkenness, his gift, his wages.
Shig-gai'on, a song of trouble, or comfort.
Shi-lo'ah. See Siloah.
Shi'loh, sent.
Shi'loh (a city), peace, abundance.
Shim'e-ah, that hears, or obeys.
Shim'e-i, that hears, or obeys, my reputation, my fame.
Shim'shai, my sun.
Shi'nar, watch of him that sleeps.
Shiph'rah, handsome, trumpet, that does good.
Shi'shak, present of the bag, of the pot, of the thigh.
Shit'tim, that turn away, or divert.
Sho'bab, returned, turned back.
Sho'bach, your bonds, your chains.
Shu'ah, pit, that swims, humiliation.
Shu'al, fox, hand, fist.
Shu'lam-ite, peaceable, perfect, that recompenses.
Shu'nem, their change, their repeating, their sleep.
Shur, wall, ox, or that beholds.
Shu'shan, lily, rose, joy.
Shu'the-lah, plant, verdure, moist pot.
Sib'mah, conversion, captivity.
Si'don, hunting, fishing, venison.
Si-gi'o-noth, according to variable songs or tunes.
Si'hon, rooting out, conclusion.
Si'hor, black, trouble. The river Nilus in Egypt.
Si'las, three, or the third.
Si'lo-ah, or Siloam, sent, a dart or branch, whatever is sent.
Sil'o-e, the same.
Sil-va'nus, who loves the forest.
Sim'e-on, that hears, that is heard.
Si'mon, that hears, that obeys.
Sin, bush.
Si'nai, a bush, enmity.
Si'on, noise, tumult.
Sir'i-on, a breastplate, deliverance.
Sis'e-ra, that sees a horse or a swallow.
Si'van, a bush or thorn.
Symr'na, myrrh.
So, a measure for grain.
So'coh, tents, tabernacles.
So'di, my secret.
Sod'om, their secret, their cement.
Sol'o-mon, peaceable, perfect.
Sop-a-ter, who defends the father.
So'rek, vine, kissing, a color inclining to yellow.
So-sip'a-ter. See Sopater.
Sos'the-ness, saviour, strong, powerful.
Spain, rare, precious.
Sta'chys, spike.
Steph'a-nas, crown, crowned.
Ste'phen, the same.
Suc'cote, tents, tabernacles.
Suc'coth-be'noth, the tabernacles of young women, or the tents of prostitutes.
Sur, that withdraws or departs.

TI

Su-san'na, lily, rose, joy.
Su'si, horse, swallow, moth.
Sy'char, a city.
Sy-e'ne, a bush, enmity.
Syn'ty-che, that speaks or discourses.
Syr'a-cuse, that draws violently.
Syr'i-a, Aram, sublime, that deceives.
Sy'ro-phe-ni-ci'i-an, drawn to, red, purple.

TA'A-NACH, who humbles thee, or who answers thee.
Tab'bath, good, goodness.
Ta'be-al, good God.
Ta'be-el, the same.
Tab'e-rah, burning.
Tab'i-tha, clear-sighted.
Ta'bor, choice, purity.
Tab'ri-mon, good pomegranate, or the navel, the middle.
Tad'mor, the palm-tree, bitterness.
Ta-hap'a-nes, secret temptation.
Tah'pe-nes, standard, flight, temptation.
Ta-li'tha-cu'mi, young woman, arise.
Tal'ma-i, my furrow, that suspends the waters, or heap of waters.
Ta'mar, palm, palm-tree.
Tam'muz, abstruse, concealed.
Tan'hu-meth, consolation, repentance.
Ta'phath, little girl, or distillation.
Tar'pel-ites, ravishers, succession of miracles.
Tar'shish, contemplation, examination of the marble.
Tar'sus, winged, feathered.
Tar'tak, chained, bound, shut up.
Tar'tan, that searches and examines the gift of the turtle.
Tat'na-i, that gives, the overseer of the gifts and tributes.
Te'bah, murder, butchery, guarding of the body, a cook.
Te'beth, the tenth month of the Hebrews.
Te'kel, weight.
Te-ko'a, a crumpet, that is confirmed.
Tel-ha'rs-a, heap, suspension of the plough.
Tel'me-lah, heap of salt, or of mariners.
Te'ma, admiration, perfection, consummation.
Te'man, the south, Africa, perfect.
Te'rah, to breathe, scent, or blow.
Ter'a-phim, an image, an idol.
Ter'ti-us, the third.
Ter-tul'lus, a liar, an impostor.
Tet'rarch, governor of a fourth part.
Thad-de'us, that praises and confesses.
Tha'hash, that makes haste, that keeps silence.
Tha'mah, that blots out, that suppresses.
The'bez, muddy, eggs, fine linen or silk.
The-laz'ar, that unbinds and grants the suspension.
The-oph'i-lus, friend of God.
Thes-sa-lo-ni'ca, victory against the Thessalonians.
Thom'as, a twin.
Thy-a-ti'ra, a perfume, sacrifice of labor.
Ti-be'ri-as, good vision, the navel.
Ti-be'ri-us, the son of Tiber.
Tib'ni, straw, hay.
Ti'dal, that breaks the yoke, knowledge of elevation.
Tig'lath-pi-le'ser, that binds or takes away captivity.
Ti-me'us, perfect, or admirable, honorable.
Tim'nath, image, figure.

TI

Ti'mon, honorable, worthy.
Ti-mo'the-us, honor of God, valued of God.
Tiph'sah, passage, leap, step, the passover.
Tir-ha-kah, inquirer, examiner, dull observer.
Tir'sha-tha, that overturns the foundation.
Tir'zah, benevolent, complaisant, well pleasing.
Tish'bite, that makes captives.
Ti'tus, honorable.
Tob, good, goodness.
Tob-a-do-ni'jah, my good God, the goodness of the foundation of the Lord.
To-bi'ah, the Lord is good.
To'gar-mah, which is all bone.
To'hu, that lives, that declares.
To'i, who wanders.
To'la, worm, grub, or scarlet.
To'phel, ruin, folly, without understanding.
To'phet, a drum, betraying.
Tro'as, penetrated.
Tro-gyl'li-um, a city in the isle of Samos.
Troph'i-mus, well educated, or well brought up.
Try-phe'na, delicious, delicate.
Try-pho'sa, thrice shining.
Tu'bal, the earth, the world, that is carried or led.
Tu'bal-ca'in, worldly possession, who is jealous of confusion.
Tych'i-cus, casual, by chance.
Ty-ran'nus, a prince, one that reigns.
Ty're, strength, rock, sharp.
Ty'rus, the same.

U'CAL, power, prevalency.
U'la-i, strength, fool, senseless.
U'lam, the porch, or the court, their strength or folly.
Ul'la, elevation, leaf, young child.
Un'ni, poor, afflicted, that answers.
Uph'az, gold of Phasis or Pison.
Ur, fire, light, a valley.
U'ri, my light, my fire.
U-ri'ah, or U-ri'jah, the Lord is my light or fire.
U'ri-el, God is my light or fire.
U'rim, and Thum'mim, light and perfection.
Uz, counsel, wood.
Uz'zah, strength, goat.
Uz'zen-she'rah, ear of the flesh.
Uz'zi, my strength, my kid.
Uz-zi'ah, the strength of the Lord.
Uz-zi'el, strength of God.

VASH'NI, the second.
Vash'ti, that drinks, or thread.
Voph'si, fragment, diminution.

ZAB'DI, portion, dowry.
Zac'che-us, pure, clean, just.
Zach-a-ri'ah, memory of the Lord.
Za'dok, just, justified.
Za'ham, crime, filthiness, impurity.
Za'ir, little, afflicted, in tribulation.
Zal'mon, his shade, his image.
Zal-mo'nah, the shades, the sound of the number, your image.
Zal-mun'na, shadow, image, or idol, forbidden.
Zam-zum'mims, projects of crimes, or enormous crimes.
Za-no'ah, forgetfulness, desertion.

23*

ZU

Zaph'nath-pa-a-ne'ah, one who discovers hidden things.
Za'rah, east, brightness.
Zar'e-phah, ambush of the mouth.
Zeb-a-di'ah, portion of the Lord, or the Lord is my portion.
Ze'bah, victim, sacrifice.
Zeb'e-dee, abundant, portion.
Ze-bo'im, deer, goat.
Ze'bul, a habitation.
Zeb'u-lun, dwelling, habitation.
Zech-a-ri'ah. See Zachariah.
Zed-e-ki'ah, the Lord is my justice, or the justice of the Lord.
Ze'eb, wolf.
Ze'lek, the shadow or the noise of him who licks or laps.
Ze-lo'phe-had, the shade or tingling of fear of being burnt.
Ze-lo'tes, jealous, full of zeal.
Zel'zah, noontide.
Ze'nas, living.
Zeph-a-ni'ah, the Lord is my secret.
Ze'phath, which beholds, that attends, or that covers.
Ze'pho, that sees and observes, that expects, or covers.
Ze'rah. See Zarah.
Zer'e-dah, ambush, change of dominion.
Ze'resh, misery, strange, or dispersed inheritance.
Ze-ror', root, that straitens or binds, that keeps tight.
Ze-ru'ah, leprous, wasp, hornet.
Ze-rub'ba-bel, a stranger at Babylon, dispersion of confusion.
Zer-u-i'ah, pain, tribulation.
Ze'thar, he that examines, or beholds.
Zi'ba, army, fight, strength.
Zib'e-on, iniquity that dwells.
Zib'i-ah, the Lord dwells.
Zich'ri, that remembers, that is a man.
Zi'don, hunting, fishing, venison.
Zif, this or that, brightness.
Zik'lag, measure pressed down.
Zil'lah, shadow, the tingling of the ear.
Zil'pah, distillation.
Zim'ran, song, singer, or vine.
Zim'ri, my field, my vine.
Zin, buckler, coldness.
Zi'on, monument, raised up, sepulchre.
Zi'or, ship of him that watches.
Ziph, this mouth, or mouthful.
Zip'por, bird, sparrow, crown, or desert.
Zip-po'rah, beauty, trumpet.
Zith'ri, to hide, demolished.
Ziz, flower, branch, or lock of hair.
Zo'an, motion.
Zo'ar, little, small.
Zo'bah, an army, or warring.
Zo'har, white, shining or dryness.
Zo'he-leth, that creeps, slides, or draws.
Zo'phar, rising early, or crown.
Zo'rah, leprosy, scab.
Zo-rob'a-bel. See Zerubbabel.
Zu'ar, small.
Zuph, that beholds, observes, or watches, roof, covering.
Zur, stone, rock, or that besieges.
Zu'-l-shad'da-i, the Almighty is my rock and strength.
Zu'zims, the posts of a door, splendor, beauty.

TABLES

OF

BIBLICAL
FACTS AND FIGURES

FOR

REFERENCE AND ILLUSTRATION.

FIVE FIRST THINGS ABOUT THE ENGLISH BIBLE.

1. First complete translation of the whole Bible was made by John Wicliffe, A.D. 1380–1382.

2. First New Testament printed in English was that of William Tyndale, A.D. 1525–1526.

3. First Bible printed in English was Miles Coverdale's, A.D. 1535.

4. First division of the Bible into verses, as we now have them, was begun by Whittingham in 1557, and completed in the Genevan Bible, 1560.

5. The Revised Version of the English Bible was begun in England June 22, 1870, and in America October 4, 1872. The New Testament was completed in England November 11, 1880, and in America October 22, 1880.

The Holy Bible is now printed in 226 different languages and dialects. There is said to be about 915 different languages and dialects spoken in the world.

THE BIBLE is said to contain 66 books, 1,189 chapters, 31,173 verses, 773,692 words, and 3,586,489 letters.

The middle verse is the 8th verse of the 118th Psalm.

The longest verse is the 9th verse of the 8th chapter of Esther.

The shortest verse is the 35th verse of the 11th chapter of St. John.

PERIODS OF THE BIBLE.

I. Embraces time from the Creation to the Deluge, or from 4004 to 2348 B.C.

II. Embraces time from the Deluge to the Death of Joseph, or from 2347 to 1635 B.C.

III. Embraces time from Joseph's Death to the Death of Moses, or from 1635 to 1451 B.C.

IV. From Death of Moses and Entrance into Canaan to the Anointing of Saul, or from 1451 to 1096 B.C.

V. Embraces the Reigns of Saul, David, and Solomon, o from 1095 to 975 B.C.

VI. **Reigns of the Kings of Judah and Israel** or from 975 to 606 **B.C.**

VII. **Embraces the Captivity and Return of the Jews**, or from **606 to 400 B.C.**

VIII. **Embraces the First Century of the Christian era.**

THE TALMUD.

The *Talmud* is a book held in esteem among the Jews, quite equal if not superior to the Sacred Scriptures. It constitutes their law as to religion and morals. The word signifies *doctrine.* The Talmud consists properly of two parts : the text, which is termed the *Mishna*, and the various commentaries of scholars on the text, called the *Gemara.* The Mishna or text, the Jews claim, was derived from Moses, by tradition through the priesthood. The Gemara is of two kinds : that of Jerusalem, and that of Babylon ; the latter being held in much the highest esteem. The former was compiled in the third century of the Christian era, and the latter, in the fifth. With many truthful doctrines, and many moral precepts of value, the Talmud contains a vast amount of idle traditions, worthless fables and frivolous injunctions, by which traditions Jesus declared the law of God had been made of none effect by the Jews. The work is useful in illustrating the doctrines and usages of the Jews, especially in the time of Christ.

THE BIBLE DISSECTED.

The following facts, taken from Horne's "Introduction," were published during the last century, by an obscure individual, three years of whose life are said to have been occupied in ascertaining them:[*]

BOOKS OF THE BIBLE.

Books in the O. T., 39 ; in the N. T., 27 ; total, 66.

Chapters in the O. T., 929 ; in the N. T., 260 ; total, 1,189.

Verses in the O. T., 23,214 ; in the N. T., 7,959 ; total, 31,173.

Words in the O. T., 592,439 ; in the N. T., 181,253 ; total, 773,692

Letters in the O. T., 2,728,800 ; in the N. T., 838,380 ; total, 3,567, 180.

APOCRYPHA.

Chapters, 183 ; verses, 6,081 ; words, 252,185.

OTHER FACTS.

The middle chapter and the least in the Bible is Ps. 117.

The middle verse is the 8th of Ps. 118th.

---

[*] Horne's "Introduction," vol. 1., p. 202, *Note.* New York Ed., 1844.

The middle line is 2d Chronicles, 4th chap., 16th verse.
The word *and* occurs in the O. T. 35,543 times.
The word *and* occurs in the N. T. 10,684 times.
The word *Jehovah* occurs 6,855 times.

OLD TESTAMENT.

The middle book is Proverbs.
The middle chapter is Job, 29th.
The middle verse is 2 Chronicles, 20th ch., 17 and 18 vv.
The least verse is 1 Chronicles, 1st ch., 25th v.

NEW TESTAMENT.

The middle book is 2 Thessalonians.
The middle chapter is Romans, 13th and 14th.
The middle verse is Acts 17th, 17th verse.
The least verse is John 11th, 35th verse.
The 21st verse of the 7th ch. of Ezra contains all the letters of the alphabet except *j*.
The 19th ch. of 2 Kings, and the 37th ch. of Isaiah are alike.

AUTHORSHIP AND DATE.

The authorship of several of the books of the Old Testament is uncertain, or positively unknown. The probabilities are largely in favor of those whose names are appended. Some of them were evidently collated and put in order by a later hand than that which made the original record. Of the authorship of the books of the New Testament, however, there can be but little question. But any uncertainty in any case on this point in no way militates against the genuineness or authority of such books as sacred records.

As to the date of their composition, certainty can not be attained. In the Old Testament the book of Job is most likely the oldest, and probably was written some 1550 B.C., while Genesis and Exodus probably bear date 1500 B.C. From those dates they range down to Malachi, about 420 B.C. As to the New Testament, the Gospel of Matthew was probably written about A.D. 58, and the Apocalypse about A.D. 96. The exact dates can not be obtained and are not essential.

HEBREW MILITARY MATTERS.

The number of the Israelites in the wilderness, of men bearing arms, was 603,550, besides 22,300 Levites; making a total of 625,850.

At *three* different times was the Census taken. On leaving Egypt, as, in Ex. xii. 37, the number being 600,000. One year after, as in

Numbers, Ch. I., with 603,550. On entering Canaan, as in Num., Ch 26, with 601,730. To this body of militia may be added the families making a total population, variously estimated, of from 2,500,000 to 3,000,000.*

Until the time of the Kings, there was no standing army, but the men were called to military service as occasion required. Saul organized a bodyguard, as the germ of an army, consisting of 3,000 men ; 2,000 with himself, and 1,000 with his son Jonathan, as his lieutenant. 1 Sam. xiii. 2. It was probably in the time of Saul that 44,760 valiant men of the tribes of Reuben and Gad, and the half tribe of Manasseh, made war on the Hagarites, (more of a pastoral than a military people,) conquered them, taking 100,000 captives, and for spoil 50,000 camels, 250,000 sheep, and 2,000 she asses. 1 Chron. v. 19–21. The same three tribes subsequently furnished 120,000 for the army of David at Hebron. 1 Chron. xii. 37.

An army of 340,800 men trained to war, came to David at Hebron to ratify his accession to the throne, after the death of Saul. 1 Chron. xii. 23–37. After his establishment in the kingdom, he had an army recruited from ten tribes of 1,570,000 ; from the tribe of Judah alone 470,000, and from the other nine tribes 1,100,000, the tribes of Levi and Benjamin not being reckoned. 1 Chron. xxi. 5.† At the same time there was an available military reserve beside, of 288,000. 1 Chron. xxvii. 1.

Abijah, King of Judah, brought into the field 400,000 chosen men against Jeroboam, King of Israel, with 800,000 chosen men. In the sanguinary conflict that followed, Jeroboam was defeated, with the slaughter of 500,000 of his soldiers in a single battle. 2 Chron. xiii. 3, 17.

King Asa had an army of 580,000 men, from the tribes of Judah and Benjamin alone, 300,000 from the former, and 280,000 from the latter. With these forces he conquered an army of Ethiopians under Zerah, of 1,000,000, with 300 war chariots. 2 Chron. xiv. 8, 9.

Jehoshaphat had an army from Judah and Benjamin of 1,160,000,

---

* See Horne's "Introduction," vol. 2, p. 86. Also Ainsworth, Roberts, and Adam Clark on Num. I., Dr. Smith's Old Testament Hist., pp. 179, 180.

† The census as given in 2 Sam. xxiv. 9, differs widely from these figures, being for Judah 500,000, and for the other tribes 800,000, a total of 1,300,000, or less than the other statement by 270,000. The larger number, however is none too large to compare with other statistics. The discrepancy has no doubt originated with careless copyists.

from the former of 780,000, and from the latter of 380,000. 2 Chron xvii. 14-18.*

How such immense armies could have been furnished and maintained on such limited territory, seems a mystery. The face of the country was illy adapted to the use of cavalry, and still more so to the use of chariots of war; except, perhaps, on the great central plain of Esdraelon, on the Syrian frontier, and along the maritime plain of Sharon, in the vicinity of Philistia. Warfare was resorted to rather for defence, than for aggression and conquest, and infantry was mainly relied on. But David reserved one hundred chariots taken as spoil from the Syrians—2 Sam. viii. 4; and Solomon had 1,400 of these chariots, with 4,000 horses for them, with an available corps of 12,000 horsemen—1 Kings x. 26; 2 Chron. i. 14.

THE SEASONS OF PALESTINE.

JANUARY.—Country verdant with young corn. Groves and meadows adorned with many flowers; oranges begin to ripen. Heavy rains; thunder storms; occasional snow, and thin ice; ground never frozen.

FEBRUARY.—Almond trees and peach trees in blossom. In the lower and warmer parts, orange trees laden with ripe fruit. Heavy rains in January and February, called by the Arabs the "fathers of rains."

MARCH.—All trees in full leaf, many in bloom. In the low lands, orange and lemon trees laden with fruits; palm trees blossom; barley ripening. Rains, hurricanes, sometimes snow. Rivers much swollen.

APRIL.—Fruits of oleaster and white mulberry; barley harvest; wheat harvest begins. Occasional rains. Sometimes sirocco from the southeast.

MAY.—*Principal harvest month.* Especially wheat, apricots, and apples ripen. In the Jordan valley vegetation withered and burnt up. Rain very seldom. From this to September, no rain occurs.

JUNE.—Almonds ripe. Honey of the Jordan valley collected in May, June, and July; grapes begin to ripen. Frequent hot winds; simoons; air motionless.

JULY.—Various fruits; apples, pears, plums, etc.; grapes fully ripe; pumpkins; harvest of corn in the higher mountains. Greatest heat in general; sky serene.

AUGUST.—*Principal fruit month.* Grapes, figs, etc.; in the plains,

---

* These figures are so large as to have seemed to some incredible. Many scholars have supposed an error in transcription. But the best authorities MSS., and Versions go to sustain the statement as it stands in the text.

walnuts and olives. Dew begins to fall; at times, large and dense "Nile clouds."

SEPTEMBER.—*Commencement of vintage.* Harvest of the dourra and maize; cotton and pomegranate begins. Much lightning, with out thunder; rain very rarely.

OCTOBER.—*End of vintage.* Gathering of cotton; plowing and sowing begin; pistachio nuts ripen. Dews very heavy; autumnal rains begin.

NOVEMBER.—*Month of plowing and sowing.* Rice harvest; fig trees laden with fruit; orange and citron trees in bloom. Rainy month; thunder-storms; rain from the west or southwest.

DECEMBER.—Trees lose their leaves; the brown and desolate plains and deserts become green pastures. The rains set in; in December, January, and February, greatest amount of rain during the year.

HEBREW FEASTS.

There were *three* great annual festivals among the Jews, at which all the males were required to "appear before the Lord," in the holy city.

The Passover.—This commemorated the deliverance of the Hebrews from Egypt, and typified the death of Christ, the Lamb of God, for the deliverance of his people. It was held *seven days*, from the 14th of Nisan, the first month of the sacred year, on which day the paschal lamb was killed, to the 21st day. It is also called the Feast of Unleavened Bread, because no leaven was allowed during its continuance.

The Pentecost.—The pentecost, or *fiftieth*, called also the Feast of Weeks. This was held *one day*, seven weeks, or a "week of weeks," after the first day of the passover. It commemorated the giving of the Law, celebrated the first fruits of the incoming harvest, and typified the outpouring of the Spirit, and the first fruits of the world's great spiritual harvest.

The Tabernacles.—This was held *eight days*, from the 15th to the 23d days of Tisri, the seventh month of the sacred year. It commemorated the dwelling of the Hebrews in tents in the wilderness, and was, therefore, sometimes called the Feast of Tents. During its observance the people were to dwell in tents and booths. It also celebrated the full ingathering of the harvest, and was the most joyous occasion of the year. It typified the wanderings of God's spiritual people, and the final ingathering of his spiritual harvest. The octave, or eighth day, was "the last, that great day of the feast.'

Various other, but less important, feasts were observed.

CHRONOLOGY OF THE ACTS OF THE APOSTLES.*

A.D. 33.—Ascension of Christ ; outpouring of the Spirit at Pentecost ; many conversions ; Pilate is still procurator ; Tiberius is Emperor until A.D. 37.

A.D. 33–35.—Peter and John heal the lame man, and are arrested ; death of Ananias and Sapphira ; deacons appointed ; martyrdom of Stephen.

A.D. 36.—Persecution scatters the church ; Philip preaches in Samaria ; Simon Magus ; baptism of the Eunuch ; Gospel preached in Phœnicia, Cyprus, and at Antioch, in Syria ; conversion of Saul.

A.D. 37–39.—Paul preaches *three years* in Damascus and in Arabia ; others spread the Gospel in Judea and Galilee ; Caligula becomes Emperor A.D. 37.

A.D. 39.—Paul escapes from Damascus, and goes to Jerusalem for the *first* time since his conversion ; he remains fifteen days, and departs for Tarsus.

A.D. 40–43.—Paul preaches in Syria and Cilicia ; Barnabas brings him to Antioch ; Peter visits Joppa, Lydda, and Cæsarea ; Dorcas is restored to life ; Cornelius baptized , Claudius becomes Emperor A.D 41 ; he makes Herod Agrippa I. king of all Palestine.

A.D. 44.—Paul labors "a whole year" with Barnabas at Antioch ; James the Elder beheaded ; Peter cast into prison ; Herod Agrippa dies at Cæsarea ; Judea governed by procurators.

A.D. 45.—Paul goes to Jerusalem the *second* time with Barnabas, to carry alms ; returns to Antioch ; goes out with Barnabas and Mark, on their *first* mission to the heathen.

A.D. 46–47.—Paul absent about *two years ;* returns by way of Perga, Attalia, to Antioch in Syria.

A.D. 48–49.—Paul remains at Antioch, probably about *two years,* preaching in the regions round about.

A.D. 50.—Apostolic conference at Jerusalem ; Paul visits Jerusalem the *third* time ; returns to Antioch with the "decrees"; Paul and Barnabas separate.

A.D. 51–54.—Paul's *second* missionary journey, Silas, Timothy, and Luke with him ; in Corinth remained *a year and a half ;* arraigned before Gallio ; while here wrote the First and Second Epistles to Thessalonians ; leaves Corinth ; returns to Cæsarea ; goes up to Jerusalem the *fourth* time ; thence to Antioch. This journey occupied about *three and a half years.* Felix becomes procurator of

---

* From Dr. Hackett's Commentary on the Acts of the Apostles.

Judea A.D. 52; Herod Agrippa II. was made king A.D. 53; in A.D. 54 Nero succeeded Claudius as Emperor.

A. D. 54–57.—Paul enters on his *third* mission to the Gentiles spends about *three years* in Ephesus; certain disciples of John baptized; the exorcists defeated; uproar about Diana; wrote his Epistle to the Galatians; First to the Corinthians, the First to Timothy, and that to Titus, as is supposed.

A.D. 58–59.—Paul visits Macedonia, where he writes his Second Epistle to the Corinthians; visits Illiricum and Corinth, and writes his Epistle to the Romans; returns to Troas; stops at Miletus; lands at Ptolemais; thence to Cæsarea; thence to Jerusalem, for his *fifth* and last visit to that city. This whole journey occupied about *four years.*

A.D. 58 or 59.—At Jerusalem Paul assumes a vow; is arrested in the Temple; rescued by Lysias; speaks to the mob; pleads citizenship, and escapes the torture; brought before the Sanhedrim; sent as a state prisoner to Felix at Cæsarea.

A. D. 59–61.—Paul kept a prisoner at Cæsarea for *two years*; pleads his cause before Felix; compelled to appeal to Cæsar; appears before King Agrippa and Felix; Festus supersedes Felix in A.D. 60 or 61.

A. D. 62–64.—Paul embarked for Rome in A.D. 60 or 61; kept in custody at Rome *two years;* during this time he wrote the Epistles to the Ephesians, Colossians, Philippians, Philemon, and—if he suffered martyrdom at this time—the Second Epistle to Timothy. The Epistle to the Hebrews was probably written at this time. Most of those who maintain that Paul was twice imprisoned at Rome, suppose that he wrote the First Epistle to Timothy, and that to Titus, during the interval between the first and second captivity; and the Second Epistle to Timothy after his second arrest, and in near prospect of his execution.*

THE RIVER JORDAN.

The Jordan is the one river of Palestine, though it has several inconsiderable tributaries, as the Jabbok and the Hieromax, which enter it from the east. The Kishon flows westward into the Mediterranean Sea near Cape Carmel. The Arnon flows westward from the mountains of Moab into the Dead Sea. But these are simply brooks, and in a land where streams abounded, would receive no other name.

The Jordan is in some respects the most remarkable river in the

---

This view Dr. Hackett thinks the correct one.

world. The religious associations connected with its history are of transcendent interest, while some of its physical features command universal regard. It has its rise about the base of the great Mt. Hermon, in or beyond the extreme north of Palestine, and running south through the Lakes Merom and Tiberias, empties into the Dead Sea.

From its sources to Lake Huleh, or Merom, is about 30 miles. From Lake Huleh to the Lake of Tiberias, or Sea of Galilee, is 10 miles. From the Sea of Galilee to the Dead Sea, in a direct line, is 60 miles. But so winding is the course of the river, that it flows no less than 200 miles to make the 60 miles of direct distance.

It flows in a deep channel, between lofty banks; passes through the Lakes Huleh and Tiberias without mingling with their waters; and hastens with a rapid current to its destination.

Its entire length would, therefore, be: from its sources to Huleh, 30 miles; through Huleh, 8 miles; to Tiberias, 10 miles; through Tiberias, 12 miles; to the Dead Sea, 200 miles. Total, 260 miles. The entire distance in a right line being about 120 miles only.

According to Van de Velde, the sources of the Jordan in the vicinity of Dan lie 650 feet above the Mediterranean Sea level. Lake Huleh is 120 feet above that level; the Sea of Galilee being 650* fee. and the Dead Sea 1,313 feet below that level, according to Lieut. Lynch. So that this remarkable river descends about 2,000 feet in 120 miles; and is rightly named the *Descender.*

Lieut. Lynch gives the width of the river as varying from 75 to 200 feet, and its depth at from 3 to 12 feet, the latter being the depth at the bathing place of the Pilgrims, in the vicinity of Jericho.

Its great descent would make a rapid current, and many falls a matter of necessity. Between Lake Tiberias and the Dead Sea, ' dashes over 27 appalling rapids, beside others of less descent." discharges daily about 6,500,000 tons of water into the Dead Sea. Its waters are sweet and healthful, and abound with fish, as de th lakes through which it passes.

THE LAKES OF PALESTINE.

Lake Huleh, or the waters of Merom, lies in the extreme northern part, some *thirty miles* from the base of the Lebanon Mountains, is irregular in shape, 8 miles in length by 6 miles in breadth.

Lake Gennesaret, Tiberias, or the Sea of Galilee, is *ten miles* south of Huleh, and is 12 miles long by 6 miles wide.

* According to the Palestine Exploration Survey it is 682 feet below.

Lake Asphaltites, or the Dead Sea, is *sixty miles* south oi the Sea of Galilee, in the southern part of the land, and is 40 miles long by 8 miles wide.

Huleh is 120 feet above* the level of the Mediterranean Sea ; the Sea of Galilee is 650 feet, and the Dead Sea 1,313 feet below that level.

JEWISH PROSELYTES.

Proselytes were converts from idolatry to the Jewish faith, and are usually reckoned of two kinds.

1. *Proselytes of the Gate.* These were persons who abandoned idolatry, accepted the faith and worship of Jehovah as the one only true God ; adopting the "Seven Precepts of Noah" as their creed ; but did not receive circumcision, nor attempt to keep the ritual law of Moses.

2. *Proselytes of Righteousness.* These were such converts to the faith as became Jews in all but birth. They were circumcised—and also baptized, as is claimed—and entered into covenant to keep the entire law of Moses, including all its ritual observances.†

THE SEVEN PRECEPTS OF NOAH.

1. That men should abstain from idolatry.
2. That they should worship the true God alone.
3. That they should abhor incest.
4. That they should not commit homicide.
5. That they should not steal or rob.
6. That they should punish murder with death.
7. That they should not eat blood, nor things strangled.‡

HOURS OF THE DAY.

The Day was reckoned from Sunrise, or 6 o'clock in the morning, and the night from Sunset, or 6 o'clock at evening ; each being divided into twelve equal parts, called the 1st, 2d, 3d, 4th, etc., hours. The 3d hour would be 9 o'clock, and the 6th hour 12 o'clock.

---

* Van de Velde, Stanley, and various other authorities give Huleh as 50 feet above the sea level. This, however, is not accepted by Dr. Smith and others, and is evidently a mistake.

† See Kitto's and Smith's Bib. Dicts., *et al.* So Lardner's Works, Vol vi., pp. 523-533.

‡ See Jahn's Bib. Archae., Sec. 325, p. 413.

WATCHES OF THE NIGHT

The Jews, like the Romans, divided the night into *four watches.*
The 1st watch.—From Sunset, or 6, to the 3d hour.
The 2d watch.—From the 3d to the 6th hour
The 3d watch.—From the 6th to the 9th hour.
The 4th watch.—From the 9th to the 12th hour, or Sunrise.

SEASONS OF THE YEAR.

1. *Seedtime ;* October and November.
2. *Winter ;* December and January.
3. *Cold Season ;* February and March.
4. *Harvest ;* April and May.
5. *Summer ;* June and July.
6. *Hot Season ;* August and September.

The expression, "Seedtime and harvest, cold and heat, summer and winter," indicates these six seasons. *Gen.* viii. 22.

The "early rain" occurs during October and November ; the "latter rain" during February and March.*

HEBREW CALENDAR.†

Sacred Year.	Civil Year.	
1. Abib, or Nisan,	April.	7.
2. Zif, or Jjar,	May.	8.
3. Sivan,	June.	9.
4. Thamus,	July.	10.
5. Ab,	August.	11.
6. Elul,	September.	12.
7. Tisri,	October.	1.
8. Bul,	November.	2.
9. Chisleu,	December.	3.
10. Tebath,	January.	4.
11. Sebat,	February.	5.
12. Adar,	March.	6.

* See Treas. Bib. Knowl., Art. Seasons.

† The months of the Hebrew Calendar correspond, not exactly out only proximately, to those of our own.